# THE PLAY THAT GOES WRONG

BY **HENRY LEWIS, JONATHAN SAYER & HENRY SHIELDS**

★

★

DRAMATISTS
PLAY SERVICE
INC.

## NOTE ON BILLING

Anyone receiving permission to produce THE PLAY THAT GOES WRONG is required to give credit to the Authors as sole and exclusive Authors of the Play on the title page of all programs distributed in connection with performances of the Play and in all instances in which the title of the Play appears, including printed or digital materials for advertising, publicizing or otherwise exploiting the Play and/or a production thereof. Please see your production license for font size and typeface requirements.

Be advised that there may be additional credits required in all programs and promotional material. Such language will be listed under the "Additional Billing" section of production licenses. It is the licensee's responsibility to ensure any and all required billing is included in the requisite places, per the terms of the license.

## SPECIAL NOTE ON SONGS/RECORDINGS

Dramatists Play Service neither holds the rights to nor grants permission to use any songs or recordings mentioned in the Play. Permission for performances of copyrighted songs, arrangements or recordings mentioned in this Play is not included in our license agreement. The permission of the copyright owner(s) must be obtained for any such use. For any songs and/or recordings mentioned in the Play, other songs, arrangements, or recordings may be substituted provided permission from the copyright owner(s) of such songs, arrangements or recordings is obtained; or songs, arrangements or recordings in the public domain may be substituted.

THE PLAY THAT GOES WRONG was first presented by Mischief Theatre under the title *The Murder Before Christmas* on December 4, 2012, at the Old Red Lion Theatre, Islington, London. It was directed by Mark Bell, the designer was Henry Lewis, the lighting design was by Scott Pryce-Jones, the costume design was by Bryony Myers, the stage manager was Thomas Platt, and the general manager was Nicholas Thompson. The cast was as follows:

| | |
|---|---|
| CHRIS | Henry Shields |
| JONATHAN | Stephen Leask |
| ROBERT | Henry Lewis |
| DENNIS | Jonathan Sayer |
| SANDRA | Charlie Russell |
| MAX | Dave Hearn |
| ANNIE | Nancy Zamit |
| TREVOR | Rob Falconer |

The production then extended under the title THE PLAY THAT GOES WRONG on March 12, 2013, with the following cast changes:

| | |
|---|---|
| JONATHAN | Henry Lewis |
| ROBERT | Greg Tannahill |
| SANDRA | Lotti Maddox |

The production then transferred to Trafalgar Studios on April 30, 2013, with the following cast changes:

| | |
|---|---|
| JONATHAN | Joshua Elliott |
| ROBERT | Henry Lewis |

The production extended at Trafalgar Studios with the following cast change:

| | |
|---|---|
| JONATHAN | Greg Tannahill |

It subsequently opened in a two-act version under the title THE PLAY THAT GOES WRONG at the Duchess Theatre, London, a Nimax Theatre, on September 14, 2014. Kenny Wax & Stage Presence presented the Mischief Theatre production. It was directed by Mark Bell, the set design was by Nigel Hook, the lighting design was by Ric Mountjoy, the costume design was by Roberto Surace, the original music was by Rob Falconer, and the sound design was by Andy Johnson. The opening night cast was as follows:

| | |
|---|---|
| TREVOR | Rob Falconer |
| CHRIS | Henry Shields |
| JONATHAN | Greg Tannahill |
| ROBERT | Henry Lewis |
| DENNIS | Jonathan Sayer |
| SANDRA | Charlie Russell |
| MAX | Dave Hearn |
| ANNIE | Nancy Zamit |
| JILL & FEMALE UNDERSTUDY | Alys Metcalf |
| PHIL & MALE UNDERSTUDY | Leonard Cook |

THE PLAY THAT GOES WRONG opened on Broadway at the Lyceum Theatre, a Shubert Theatre, in April 2017. It was produced by Kevin McCollum, J.J. Abrams, Kenny Wax, Stage Presence Ltd., Catherine Schreiber, Ken Davenport, Double Gemini Productions/deRoy-Brunish, Damian Arnold/TC Beech, Greenleaf Productions/Bard-Roth, Martian Entertainment/Jack Lane/John Yonover, Lucas McMahon, and Mischief Theatre. It was directed by Mark Bell, the scenic design was by Nigel Hook, the costume design was by Roberto Surace, the lighting design was by Ric Mountjoy, the sound design was by Andrew Johnson, the associate costume designer was Lisa Zinni, the associate lighting designer was Jeremy Cunningham, and the associate sound designer was Beth Lake. The opening night cast was as follows:

| | |
|---|---|
| TREVOR | Rob Falconer |
| MAX | Dave Hearn |
| ROBERT | Henry Lewis |
| SANDRA | Charlie Russell |
| DENNIS | Jonathan Sayer |
| CHRIS | Henry Shields |
| JONATHAN | Greg Tannahill |
| ANNIE | Nancy Zamit |
| UNDERSTUDIES | Matthew Cavendish (CHRIS, DENNIS, JONATHAN, MAX, TREVOR) |
| | Bryony Corrigan (ANNIE, SANDRA) |
| | Adam Daveline (CHRIS, DENNIS, MAX, ROBERT, TREVOR) |
| | Jonathan Fielding (CHRIS, DENNIS, JONATHAN, MAX, ROBERT) |
| | Amelia McClain (ANNIE, SANDRA, TREVOR) |
| | Greg Tannahill (ROBERT) |
| | Michael Thatcher (JONATHAN, ROBERT, TREVOR) |

# CHARACTERS

*As with any play-within-a-play, you have the complication of the characters of the actors doing the play-within-the-play and the characters within the play-within-the-play. To make it a little simpler, the names are laid out below in two lists: firstly the members of the Cornley Drama Society who are putting on the play, and secondly the characters of* The Murder at Haversham Manor. *The text always uses the actors' names rather than the characters' names.*

## MEMBERS OF THE CORNLEY DRAMA SOCIETY
*(in order of appearance)*

ANNIE is the company's stage manager. American accent.

STAGE CREW, the Cornley Drama Society stage crew.

TREVOR is the company's lighting and sound operator. American accent.

CHRIS is the head of the drama society, directed the play and plays Inspector Carter.

JONATHAN plays Charles Haversham.

ROBERT plays Thomas Colleymoore.

DENNIS plays Perkins.

MAX plays Cecil Haversham and Arthur the Gardener.

SANDRA plays Florence Colleymoore.

*The action takes place on the opening night of the Cornley Drama Society's production of* The Murder at Haversham Manor *by Susie H. K. Brideswell. Present day.*

## CHARACTERS IN *THE MURDER AT HAVERSHAM MANOR*
*(in order of appearance)*

CHARLES HAVERSHAM, the deceased.

THOMAS COLLEYMOORE, Charles' old school friend.

PERKINS, Charles' butler.

CECIL HAVERSHAM, Charles' brother.

FLORENCE COLLEYMOORE, Charles' fiancée and Thomas' sister.

INSPECTOR CARTER, an esteemed local inspector.

ARTHUR THE GARDENER, the gardener at Haversham Manor.


*The action takes place in Charles' private rooms at Haversham Manor on the evening of Charles and Florence's engagement party. Winter 1922.*


## SCRIPT NOTES

The stage direction "vamp" indicates improvised dialogue or action.

A forward slash / denotes the next line beginning midway through the current line.

# PERFORMANCE NOTES

The preshow and interval activity should be subtle, incidental and not draw the full attention of the audience. The show should not feel like it's begun until Trevor addresses the whole audience.

A crucial thing to remember when performing this piece is to tell the story of *The Murder at Haversham Manor*. That is what the actors of Cornley are setting out to do and as such should be what the cast of *The Play That Goes Wrong* are setting out to do. The characters of the actors you will no doubt work on in detail, but their temperaments and flaws should shine through the cracks in their performances and not suffocate the action. Always try to tell the murder mystery story and play the *Haversham Manor* characters. Without that solid structure to support the comedy, the show will unravel.

Everything in the show must of course be played for truth and not for laughs or parody. For Cornley this show is not a comedy, it's a serious play, and it is so important to them all that it goes well, so when it goes wrong it hurts.

We've also found it useful to remember that the actors of the Cornley Drama Society are not bad actors but the victims of unfortunate circumstance. The comedy comes from their unwavering endeavour to continue, their bad choices in trying to get out of the situations they find themselves in and their optimistic belief that their luck will change.

The same is true of the set, costumes, lighting, sound and all other elements of the production. Everything that goes wrong should be a choice, and everything that doesn't go wrong should go perfectly or (in the case of the physical production) look perfect. The better the production looks, the more of a journey there is to the complete destruction that occurs in the later stages of the play.

In essence it is vital everyone works to present "the play that goes wrong," not "the play that's being done badly."

# THE PLAY THAT GOES WRONG

## ACT ONE

*The setting is the private rooms of Charles Haversham, a young, wealthy man of the period. The rooms occupy a whole wing of "Haversham Manor" and are split onto two levels.*

*The ground floor consists of a lounge area. There is a fireplace s. r. with a cartouche at its top center. A picture of a King Charles spaniel hangs above the fireplace, two swords hang in the hearth and a coal scuttle stands s. l. of the fireplace. There is a large window in the centre of the stage with red velvet curtains closed over it and a grandfather clock to the left of it, with the time set to five o'clock. There is a door in between the window and the fireplace; the funnel of a voice pipe and a barometer hang on either side of it. A large heraldic shield hangs above the door.*

*A chaise longue littered with cushions stands D.S. C. on a large rug. A small table stands D.S. R. with a telephone and a vase of flowers on it. D.S. L. is another small table, set with a silver tray with four short glasses on it. A chandelier hangs in the centre of the lounge. A contemporary tool kit is D.S. C.*

*On the s. l. side are a number of bookcases packed with books and above them the upper level of the set: Charles' study. There is a small round window on the u.s. wall of the study, beneath which sits a desk and chair. On the s. r. side of the round window is a safe set into the wall, and on the s. l. side of the desk stands a tall pot plant. There is a door to the study on the s. l. side and double doors to an elevator D.S. of that. Corresponding elevator double doors stand directly below the upper level. Beneath the D.S. R. corner of the upper level is a pillar extending down to the ground to support the weight of the platform. In between the upstairs door and the upstairs elevator doors stands a globe-style drinks cabinet, above which hangs another voice pipe funnel.*

*Set apart from the stage is a tech box complete with computer, faders and littered with empty drinks cans, etc. The tech box is visible to the audience and is where Trevor will be seen operating lights and sound for the show.*

*Dramatic house music plays.*

PRESHOW ACTIVITY:

*As the audience enter, Trevor is finishing off laying the floorboards U.S. R. under the upper level. His hammer breaks.*

*Two members of the stage crew are searching the stalls and circle for a missing Duran Duran CD\* and for Winston, a dog needed for later in the show.*

*Chris greets members of the audience as they arrive, in his best tuxedo.*

*Annie is by the fireplace trying to stick a mantelpiece above it and trying to stick an old journal to the mantelpiece. She enlists the help of an audience member and gets them to hold the mantelpiece in place before disappearing offstage. Trevor appears and commandeers the audience member to sweep the stage. As they start sweeping, the head of the broom falls off. Annie reappears and brings the audience member back to help with the mantelpiece. She sends them to get her tool kit. The audience member can't lift it. After several attempts Annie crosses over and picks it up easily. The mantelpiece is eventually stuck in position over the fireplace, and the audience member is sent back to their seat.*

*Trevor comes D.S. C. Annie scuttles off.*

TREVOR.  Good evening, ladies and gentle—

---

\* If music by a different band is used on pages 45 and 78, adjust this activity appropriately.

*The mantelpiece falls off the wall. Annie emerges from the wing.*

ANNIE. *(To the audience member.)* You said that was fine.

TREVOR. *(Aside to Annie.)* Just leave it, leave it.

> *Annie starts to try and repair the mantelpiece. Trevor addresses the audience.*

Okay, welcome to *The Murder at Haversham Manor*. Can I kindly request that all your cell phones and other electronic devices are switched off and please note that photography of any kind is strictly prohibited. Also if anyone finds a Duran Duran* CD box set anywhere in the auditorium, that is a personal item and I want that back. Please do drop it at my tech box end of the show. Enjoy the performance.

> *House and stage lights go down. Trevor exits s. l.*

*(On his radio but broadcast to the whole theatre.)* Alright, can we prepare for lights up on Act One, note for the cast Winston is still missing, we need to find him before the guard dog scene—

CHRIS. Trevor! Trevor!

TREVOR. *(Still over the speakers.)* —we need him back in his cage as soon as possible. What's Annie doing onstage? Get her off so Chris can do his stupid speech—*oop!*

> *Trevor's microphone cuts off. Annie hasn't finished repairing the mantelpiece. Chris enters from the s. r. wing in the darkness.*

CHRIS. Leave it. Just leave it.

ANNIE. You need it…

CHRIS. We don't have time.

> *Annie hurries off into the wings, taking the mantelpiece and tool kit with her. Spotlight comes up on Chris, cutting off his head.*

Good evening, ladies and gentlemen, and…

> *Chris steps forward into the spotlight.*

…welcome to the Cornley Drama Society's presentation of *The Murder at Haversham Manor*. Please allow me to introduce myself; I am Chris, the director, and I would like to personally welcome

---

* If music by a different band is used on pages 45 and 78, change "Duran Duran" appropriately.

you to what will be my directorial debut *(Pronounced "day-boo.")* and my first production as head of the drama society.

Firstly I would like to apologise to those of you involved in our little box office mix-up. I do hope the six hundred and seventeen of you affected will enjoy our little murder mystery just as much as you would have enjoyed *Hamilton*.

We are particularly excited to present this play because, for the first time in the society's history, we've managed to find a play that fits the number of society members perfectly. If we're honest a lack of members has sometimes hampered past productions, such as last year's Chekhov play... *Two Sisters*. Last Christmas' *The Lion and the Wardrobe*. Or indeed our summer musical, *Cat*.

Of course this will be the first time the society has been able to stage a play of this scale and we are thrilled. It's no secret we usually have to contend with a small budget, as was evident in our recent production of Roald Dahl's classic *James and the Peach*. Of course during the run of that particular show the peach we had went off, and we were forced to present a hastily devised alternative entitled *James! Where's Your Peach?*

Anyway on to the main event, which I am confident will be our best show yet! So ladies and gentlemen, without any further ado, please put your hands together—

> *If the audience start to clap too early, Chris can say "not yet."*

—for Susie H. K. Brideswell's thrilling whodunit—*The Murder at Haversham Manor*.

> *Chris exits into the s. r. wing. Spotlight down. Trevor takes up his position in his tech box. Darkness. Music.*
>
> *Jonathan (playing Charles Haversham) enters through the darkness from the s. r. wing. He trips and falls over. The lights suddenly come up on Jonathan on the floor. He freezes. The lights go out again. Jonathan takes up his position: dead on the chaise longue, with his arm outstretched onto the floor. The lights come up again just before he's fully in position.*
>
> *Knocking at the downstairs door. Robert (playing Thomas Colleymoore) and Dennis (playing Perkins the Butler) can*

*be heard behind it.*

ROBERT. *(Off.)* Charley! Are you ready? We're all waiting downstairs to raise a glass to your engagement. Charley?

*Robert knocks on the door.*

Come along now, Charley, you've been in there for hours now. If I didn't know better I'd say you were having second thoughts about the wedding. *(Chuckles.)* Charley? Hang it all, Charley, if you won't come out, we'll come in. *(Tries handle.)* Damn it, he's locked the door. Hand me those keys, Perkins.

DENNIS. *(Off.)* Here they are, Mr. Colleymoore.

ROBERT. *(Off.)* Thank you, Perkins. Let's get this door open. We're coming in, Charley! We're coming in!

*Robert tries to open the door, but it won't budge. Dennis and Robert hammer on the door to try and open it.*

*(Still off.)* There we are. We're in.

*Robert and Dennis dart around the side of the set to enter.*

But what's this? Charles, unconscious?

DENNIS. Asleep surely, Mr. Colleymoore?

ROBERT. Damn it, Perkins, I hope so.

DENNIS. I'll take his pulse.

*Dennis takes Jonathan's pulse on his forehead. Jonathan slowly tilts his head to move Dennis' fingers down onto his neck.*

ROBERT. Blast! I knew something must have been wrong, it's so unlike Charles to disappear like this.

DENNIS. Sir, he's dead!

*Lights snap to red. Dramatic musical spike. Lights snap back to the general state.*

ROBERT. Damn it, Perkins, he can't be! He's my oldest friend.

DENNIS. He's not breathing, sir, and there's no hint of a heartbeat.

ROBERT. Well I'm dumbfounded. He was right as—

*Robert crosses in front of the chaise longue, treading on Jonathan's outstretched hand.*

—*rain* an hour ago.

13

DENNIS. I don't understand. He can't be dead. He was as fit as a fiddle. It doesn't make sense.

ROBERT. Of course it makes sense. He's been murdered!

> *Lights snap to red again. The same dramatic musical spike. Lights snap back to general state.*

Good God. Where's Florence?

DENNIS. She's in the dining room, sir. Shall I fetch her?

ROBERT. At once, Perkins, and quickly.

DENNIS. But she's bound to have one of her hysterical episodes.

ROBERT. Damn it, gather everyone in here. Charles! Dead! What a horror.

> *Dennis rushes to the voice pipe on the wall and calls to the rest of the house. Robert removes his jacket.*

DENNIS. *(Into the voice pipe.)* Lounge to dining room. Cecil! Miss Colleymoore! Come to Charles' private rooms at once. Charles Haversham has been murdered.

ROBERT. But do you think it was murder, Perkins?

> *Robert hangs his jacket up on a hook on the wall.*

Or do you think perhaps—

> *The hook holding Robert's jacket falls to the floor.*

—it was suicide?

DENNIS. Suicide? Mr. Haversham? Not possible! Never was there a man with more zest for life than Charles Haversham. He was young, rich and soon to be married. Why on earth would he commit suicide?

ROBERT. But why on earth would anybody want to murder him? Charles was such a gentle fellow.

DENNIS. Generous, kind, a true… *(Reads a word written on his hand.)* philanthropist. *(Pronounced "phill-an-throp-ist.")* He never had an enemy in his life.

ROBERT. Until today it seems.

DENNIS. Shall I telephone the police, sir?

ROBERT. The police? They wouldn't make it out here for days in this snowstorm.

*Robert opens the curtains to reveal falling paper snowflakes.*

No.

*Robert closes the curtains again.*

I'll telephone Inspector Carter, he lives just the other side of the village. *(Picks up receiver.)* He'll be here in next to no time. Hand me the phone, Perkins.

*Robert realises he already has the receiver.*

Thank you, Perkins.

*Dennis sits on Jonathan's crotch.*

Good evening. Give me Inspector Carter... I know it's late... Damn it, I don't care about the weather. There's been a murder. Someone's murdered Charles Haversham!

*Lights change to red. A musical spike plays again. The lights shift back to the general state, but the music continues. It cuts out briefly.*

That's right.

*The music continues. Dennis keeps trying to get up, thinking the spike will stop, and repeatedly sits back down on Jonathan until Jonathan pushes him off.*

That's right!

TREVOR. *(Over the speakers.)* Sound effect error on cue four.

ROBERT. Thank you. *(Hangs up.)* He's on his way.

DENNIS. Inspector Carter?

ROBERT. They say he's the best damn inspector in the district, he'll crack this case and quick.

DENNIS. Very good, sir, and what shall I do?

ROBERT. Lock every door, man.

*Robert crosses the stage again. Dennis follows. Jonathan sharply moves his hand out of the way of Robert's foot. Once Robert has passed, Jonathan replaces his hand. Dennis treads on it as he follows Robert past the chaise longue.*

Not a soul gets out of Haversham Manor until the killer is found.

DENNIS. At once, sir.

ROBERT. …and assemble everyone in here.

DENNIS. Right away, sir.

*Dennis goes to leave through the door, but it still won't budge.*

ROBERT. Good God! Charles Haversham murdered at his own engagement party!

*Robert sees Dennis stuck onstage and repeats his line to stall as Dennis slowly exits around the side of the flat.*

Good God! Charles Haversham murdered at his own engagement party! What a grim, grim night. *(Turns sharply to the door.)* Florence!

*We hear a bang as Sandra tries to get in through the door.*

SANDRA. *(Off.)* Charley! No! I can't believe what I'm seeing.

*Robert goes to try and open the door. Sandra appears in the window, holding apart the curtains.*

My God, he looks so frail lying there. His skin is cold to the touch.

ROBERT. Don't touch him, Florence.

SANDRA. I must!

ROBERT. You mustn't!

SANDRA. You controlling brute, unhand me!

*Robert pretends to release Sandra's hand.*

Oh, who could do such a thing? The night of our engagement party. Cecil, quick! Your brother's dead.

DENNIS. This way, Mr. Haversham.

MAX. *(Off.)* I'm coming, Miss Colleymoore!

*We hear three loud bangs on the door. On the third the door suddenly bursts open, revealing Max, Annie and members of stage crew who had all been attempting to open it.*

ROBERT. Get out, you idiots.

*They all quickly run off.*

MAX. My brother? Dead? It can't be!

*Sandra now enters through the door.*

ROBERT. Calm yourself, Cecil. Pour him a stiff drink, Perkins.

DENNIS. Right away, sir. Charles always kept his scotch upstairs in his study.

*Dennis gets into the elevator carriage. The elevator rises to the upper-level study. Dennis emerges and walks over to the drinks cabinet.*

MAX. You know my brother had the finest collection of scotch in all the county.

ROBERT. Don't you think I know that, Cecil? He was my best friend.

MAX. Well he was my brother, Thomas.

ROBERT. Hang it all, Charley dead.

SANDRA. My fiancé dead, I can't bear it.

ROBERT. You aren't to leave my sight this evening, Florence.

*Dennis opens the drinks cabinet and takes out a full bottle of scotch.*

DENNIS. *(Into the voice pipe.)* Oh my God! He's drunk the whole bottle, sir. There's not a drop left.

ROBERT. *(Into the voice pipe.)* Hang it all, ther…

*Dennis realises and tries to get rid of the scotch, pouring it into the voice pipe. The scotch spurts out of Robert's end of the voice pipe, all over him. He quickly grabs the coal scuttle and catches the liquid inside.*

DENNIS. There's not a drop left!

*The bottle is now empty.*

ROBERT. *(Into the voice pipe.)* Hang it all, there's another in the cabinet.

*Dennis produces the empty bottle he should have got the first time from the bottom shelf of the cabinet.*

DENNIS. Yes, sir, of course you're right, this one's full.

ROBERT. This is horrifying. I mean who on earth would have a motivation to murder Charles Haversham?

*Dennis descends in the elevator, puts the bottle onto the tray of short glasses on the D.S. L. table and carries the tray past the window. As Dennis passes the window, Annie leans through and exchanges the empty bottle for a full plastic bottle labelled "WHITE SPIRIT" with a large flammable symbol on it. Dennis doesn't see the switch.*

SANDRA.  I can't imagine!

MAX.  It's madness! My brother was a good man. Who would kill him? I'm in shock, Thomas.

ROBERT.  As am I, Cecil. As am I.

MAX.  My brother murdered in his own home! This is unthinkable!

SANDRA.  This is more than my nerves can take. I simply can't stand it. Thomas, I think I'm becoming hysterical!

ROBERT.  No, Florence! Not another one of your episodes. Calm yourself. Here, take one of your pills.

MAX.  Oh Florence, this is unbearable.

> *Sandra begins to scream and pound Jonathan's chest. Jonathan flinches.*

Thomas, I feel I shall pass out.

ROBERT.  Perkins! Pour that man a stiff drink!

> *Dennis arrives d.s. r. and offers a glass to Max.*

MAX.  Thank you, Perkins.

ROBERT.  There, there, Florence, well done, deep breaths.

> *Dennis pours the white spirit into Max's glass. Sandra becomes calmer.*

SANDRA.  This is terrible, just a week after our engagement.

MAX.  Well here's to a good brother.

> *Max raises his glass and drinks the white spirit. He quickly spits it back out.*

That's the best whisky I've ever tasted.

ROBERT.  Have another, to calm your nerves.

MAX.  Make it a double!

> *Dennis pours Max another glass of white spirit.*

SANDRA.  Oh my Charles! My Charles! My head is spinning!

> *Max drinks it again. He spits it out again.*

MAX.  Calm down, Florence.

DENNIS.  Another scotch, sir?

MAX.  Yes!

SANDRA. I can't believe he was sat up here alone, drinking, when he was supposed to be downstairs with us.

> *Max drinks again and spits it out again, this time right into Jonathan's face, who sits up in shock. Beat. Robert pushes Jonathan back down onto the chaise longue.*

MAX. My…

> *He lets out a throaty squeak, the white spirit burning his mouth.*

My brother wasn't as happy as people were led to believe. Behind that cheery mask lay a darker side to the man that many didn't know about.

DENNIS. It's true, his smile was often merely *(Reads from his hand.)* a facade. *(Pronounced "fu-cayde.")* I was fortunate enough to be one of the few people who he really confided in. Damn it all, I've lost a true friend today.

ROBERT. We all have, Perkins. Hang it, I knew Charley ever since school.

SANDRA. I don't know how I'll ever recover from this.

ROBERT. You'll move back home with me. I'm your brother and I'll have it no other way.

MAX. Perkins is right, my brother was hiding a deep sense of melancholy and resentment. I have no doubt in my mind it was suicide.

DENNIS. Suicide, Mr. Haversham? How can you say that! Of course not, it's murder. Murder in the first degree.

MAX. Nonsense!

> *Max performs a gesture for "nonsense." If the audience laugh, Max can acknowledge them here by smiling and repeating the gesture.*

*Nonsense!* My brother was paranoid and jealous and I can prove it. Perkins, hand me his journal, it's there on the mantelpiece.

> *Annie's hand reaches through the door and holds the journal against the wall where it should have been above the fireplace. Dennis passes it to Max.*

Thank you, Perkins. Why, look at the last entry. *(Not looking at the journal.)* "I fear Florence does not love me. The night of our engagement party, despair engulfs my soul."

SANDRA. But I loved Charles with all my heart.

*Dennis takes the journal and puts it back where the mantel-piece should be; it falls straight to the floor. Annie's hand reaches back through the door to catch it, but she is just too late.*

MAX. As I said: driven mad with paranoia and jealousy.

*All gasp and face out. Silence. The cast wait for a sound effect that doesn't happen. Eventually Trevor realises he's missed his cue.*

TREVOR. Oh no!

*Trevor hits a button. A loud door chime sounds.*

ALL. The Inspector!

SANDRA. Thank heavens he's here.

*Chris (now in costume, playing Inspector Carter) enters through the door with paper snowflakes on his head and shoulders. He carries an attaché case.*

CHRIS. What a terrible snowstorm. Good evening, I'm Inspector Carter. Take my case.

DENNIS. Yes, Inspector.

*Chris hands his case to Dennis, who places it on the floor by the table.*

CHRIS. This must be Charles Haversham. I'm sorry. This must've given you all a damn shock.

SANDRA. It did, we're all still reeling.

CHRIS. Naturally. Tell me, are any of you the deceased's immediate family?

MAX. I'm Cecil Haversham. I'm his brother.

SANDRA. *(Smiling.)* I'm Florence Colleymoore. I'm his fiancée. Tonight was our engagement party.

CHRIS. I take it everyone is assembled in here?

ROBERT. Yes. The only other member of staff is Arthur the Gardener, but I saw him and Winston leaving for the weekend hours ago.

CHRIS. Winston?

ROBERT. His guard dog.

CHRIS. Very well. Have you poured everyone a stiff drink?

DENNIS. Yes, Inspector.

> *Dennis holds out the tray, and they all take a glass.*

MAX. Well then let's all raise a glass—

> *As the glasses are lifted, Dennis lowers the tray, hitting Jonathan on the head.*

To a man we all loved, to Charles.

ALL. Charles!

> *They all raise their glasses and drink the white spirit. They all spit it out and try to recover. Max holds the white spirit in his mouth.*

CHRIS. Delicious.

SANDRA. Excellent.

ROBERT. Lovely. That's a damn fine bottle, Perkins, what's the vintage?

DENNIS. *(Reads the label.)* Flammable and corrosive, sir.

CHRIS. *Listen!* You all must be distraught, but forgive me, the sooner I can begin my enquiries—

> *Chris deposits his notebook on the s. r. table.*

—the sooner we can get to the bottom of this ghastly business.

> *Max turns u.s. and spits out his white spirit. He turns back looking as casual as he can but then gags, giving himself away.*

*(To Dennis.)* If you'd be so kind as to take the body up to the study, so I can examine it.

DENNIS. Yes, Inspector.

ROBERT. I'll lend you a hand, Perkins.

CHRIS. Then lock all the doors to the house and prepare this room, I shall conduct my enquiries in here afterwards.

DENNIS. Inspector.

> *Over the next few lines, Dennis brings in a stretcher. Robert and Dennis lay the stretcher on the floor in front of the chaise longue.*

MAX. Any ideas as to the cause of death, Inspector?

CHRIS. Could be a number of things. Strangulation, suffocation, poison. Before fully examining the body I wouldn't like to say.

SANDRA. Poison, Inspector? Surely not.

> *Robert and Dennis try to lift Jonathan up but can't.*

CHRIS. Try not to think about it, Miss Colleymoore.

> *Robert and Dennis slowly start to roll Jonathan off of the chaise. Chris slows down his lines as he watches.*

As soon as I've...finished...up...sta...irs.

> *Jonathan opens his eyes and looks frightened. Eventually he tips off of the chaise and falls hard facedown onto the floor.*

I'll speak to everyone individually and then you can get some space to calm your nerves.

> *Robert and Dennis lift the stretcher up; the canvas tears off of the stretcher and Robert and Dennis are left holding just the poles. Beat. Robert and Dennis then carry the poles off through the door, leaving Jonathan on the floor.*

SANDRA. Thank you, Inspector, this is all more than I can bear.

CHRIS. I shall return presently, as soon as I've finished...examining the body.

> *Chris exits, slowly shutting the door behind him, staring at Jonathan as he goes. Pause.*

MAX. Well—

> *Jonathan realises that he is meant to have been carried off and suddenly starts to get up, making Max and Sandra jump slightly. They stare at Jonathan, who, trying not to be seen, exits towards the door, taking the stretcher canvas with him. He slowly leaves through the door and shuts it behind him.*

Well thank God they've all gone.

> *Lights shift to the upper level. Robert and Dennis enter through the upstairs door, carrying a mimed body.*

ROBERT. Good Lord, Perkins, this body weighs a tonne!

CHRIS. So this is Charles' private study. Set the body down there, gentlemen.

> *They put down the mimed body on the floor by the D.S. edge*

*of the upper level.*

DENNIS.  It's such a tragedy for a man to die just three months before he is to be married.

ROBERT.  I can't stand it. Just look at him lying there.

DENNIS.  This is most *(Checks hand.)* morose. *(Pronounced "more-ous.")*

ROBERT.  Morose indeed.

*Lights shift downstairs.*

SANDRA.  Cecil, we must tread carefully. It would be easy for the two of us to become implicated in Charles' death. If they find out about us, we'll be suspects.

MAX.  We were having an affair, so what? It doesn't mean—

*Max slips on a puddle of white spirit.*

It doesn't mean we killed the man.

SANDRA.  Of course not, but that's what the Inspector will think.

MAX.  It's fine, we'll just carry on as if every-*thing!*

*Max sits on the chaise longue but feels something hard under the cushions.*

—is just as it was. Except—

*Max lifts the cushions and discovers a ledger underneath. Max puts it under the chaise longue.*

Except now you won't be forced to marry my beastly brother.

SANDRA.  And soon we can be together and not keep secrets.

MAX.  Soon my love, but first, with Charley finally out of the picture I must ask you one question.

*Max goes down on one knee in front of Sandra, D.S. of the upper level. Lights shift to upstairs.*

DENNIS.  It's so strange to think of Charles being dead.

*Jonathan opens the upstairs door and creeps in, carrying the stretcher canvas with him. He moves forward to try and take up his position: dead on the floor. The others don't notice him standing behind them.*

He was such an influence on all our lives.

ROBERT. It's almost as though he's still alive in the room with us.

DENNIS. His stillness unnerves me.

CHRIS. Seeing a cadaver for the first time can be unsettl-*ing!*

> *Chris sees Jonathan and jumps in shock. Dennis and Robert let out a scream in surprise. Jonathan quietly moves in front of them and lies down on the front edge of the upper level. As he puts his head back, he bangs it on the bottom of the elevator door.*

Check his pockets, Thomas.

ROBERT. Inspector.

> *Chris produces a tin of powder and a brush.*

CHRIS. I need you to pull yourselves together and help me to dust his body for fingerprints.

> *Chris passes Dennis the tin and brush.*

DENNIS. Yes, Inspector.

> *Robert searches Jonathan's trouser pocket but cannot find the prop letter he is supposed to find. After a few moments, Jonathan reaches into his inside jacket pocket and produces the letter and passes it to Robert. Robert quickly pretends to have taken the letter from Jonathan's trouser pocket and holds it up.*

ROBERT. *A letter?*

> *Robert passes the letter to Chris, who puts it in his pocket.*

CHRIS. Now to dust the body for fingerprints.

ROBERT. What was that?

DENNIS. Sir?

ROBERT. I could have sworn I just saw him breathing.

DENNIS. Breathing, sir—

> *Dennis drops the tin of powder onto Jonathan's face. Jonathan tries to hide his coughing.*

CHRIS. Nonsense, Colleymoore. This man is dead.

> *Lights shift to downstairs. Robert, Chris and Dennis freeze in a group pose, each with their right hand on their chin.*

*Jonathan continues to cough.*

MAX. Florence, will you do me the honour of becoming my wife? Marry me!

> *Jonathan coughs again, more violently, which causes him to slip off of the upper level. He grabs hold of the edge, his legs dangling down. Robert, Dennis and Chris try to haul him back up. Vamp. After a few moments they lose their grip, and Jonathan falls down to the floor, landing in between Max and Sandra. Robert, Dennis and Chris put their hands back on their chins.*

Charles is dead. He can never come between us again.

> *Jonathan slowly gets up, retrieves the canvas, hides behind it and moves back towards the door. Unable to see, he opens the door into his own head and then exits, closing the door behind him.*

Florence, Charles is gone and he's never coming back.

> *Lights shift to upstairs. Max and Sandra freeze.*

CHRIS. Thank you, gentlemen. Now that I have finished examining the body, perhaps you would take it down to the service quarters for the coroner to collect in the morning.

DENNIS. Yes, Inspector.

> *Robert and Dennis mime lifting the body again.*

CHRIS. Check all of the doors are locked, Perkins.

DENNIS. Inspector.

CHRIS. And Colleymoore, perhaps you could fetch me a pencil and my notebook from downstairs.

ROBERT. Naturally.

> *Jonathan reenters upstairs, holding up the canvas to hide himself. He peers over the top and sees the others.*

(*Ad libs.*) After you, Charles.

> *Jonathan, Robert, Dennis and Chris exit. The lights shift downstairs as they go.*

SANDRA. Oh Cecil, I can't resist you! I shall, I shall marry you.

MAX. Oh Florence, come into my arms.

*Max pushes Sandra away.*

SANDRA.  I shall!

MAX.  Kiss me!

SANDRA.  Oh Cecil!

*Max and Sandra go to kiss, but Robert bursts in.*

ROBERT.  The Inspector requires a pencil. What on earth's going on in here?

SANDRA.  Sorry, I felt flustered. Cecil was cooling my brow.

ROBERT.  Very well, now I have the pencil I'll be on my…

*Robert sees that there is no pencil on the D.S. R. table. He picks up the set of keys instead.*

Well now I have the… well now I have the… Now I have the *pencil.* I'll be on my way.

*Robert exits, closing the door.*

MAX.  Thank God he's gone!

SANDRA.  Oh, Cecil! Kiss me a thousand times; I'm yours.

*Dennis bursts in.*

DENNIS.  Sorry to interrupt, Miss Colleymoore, Mr. Haversham. I've come to collect the keys to lock us all inside.

MAX.  Thank you, Perkins.

*Dennis sees the keys gone, and instead he picks up the Inspector's notebook.*

DENNIS.  I shall lock the doors at once.

*Dennis exits with the Inspector's notebook.*

SANDRA.  You don't think Perkins suspects us, do you?

MAX.  That old fool, of course not.

SANDRA.  Oh, enough words. Take me!

*Robert bursts in.*

ROBERT.  I forgot the Inspector's notebook… what in God's name?

SANDRA.  I was about to faint. Cecil caught me.

ROBERT.  I haven't time for this. Now…I…have…the Inspector's notebook, I'll be on my way.

> *Robert sees the notebook to be gone. He picks up the vase of flowers instead and exits.*

MAX. Damn these blasted interruptions!

SANDRA. Kiss me, Cecil, I can't wait a second longer.

> *Pause. Dennis is supposed to have burst in. Max and Sandra look at the door.*

Kiss me, Cecil, I can't wait a second longer.

> *Silence.*

Kiss me, Cecil, I can't wait a second longer.

> *Max and Sandra vamp, Sandra trying to convince Max to kiss her. Eventually Max kisses Sandra, putting his entire wide-open mouth over hers. Sandra recoils and falls off of the chaise longue. Dennis then bursts in, holding two candles in candlesticks.*

DENNIS. Sorry to interrupt, Mr. Haversham, Miss Colleymoore. I have come to prepare the room.

MAX. Thank you, Perkins. Just set them down on the mantelpiece.

> *Dennis goes to the fireplace with the candlesticks. But there is no mantelpiece to put them on. Suddenly Annie's hands burst through the fireplace. Dennis puts a candlestick in each of her hands.*

That's some good work, thank you, Perkins.

> *Dennis exits. He slams the door closed, and as he does, the cartouche on the fireplace drops to the floor and reveals Annie's face. She stares out at the others.*

At last we're alone.

> *Annie pulls the candlesticks back, but they are too tall and she can't pull them through the holes.*

SANDRA. Oh Cecil, let's run away from here. Far away! Together!

MAX. Soon, my love, but we must be careful. We mustn't arouse suspicion.

SANDRA. Cecil, tell me, who do you think killed Charles?

MAX. I have no doubt in my mind, he was killed by your brother: Thomas Colleymoore.

SANDRA. My brother a murderer and Charles dead? What a devil of a situation this is!

> *Jonathan suddenly bursts through the downstairs door, holding a gun.*

JONATHAN. Not so fast, Inspector!

> *Max and Sandra stare at Jonathan. Pause. Jonathan realises he has come in much too early. He exits.*

SANDRA. But why would Thomas want Charles dead?

MAX. Isn't it obvious? He—

> *Max turns and walks u.s., hitting his head on the pillar underneath the upper level.*

*Argh!* He was always bitter and possessive when it came to you!

> *Throughout the following dialogue, Max begins miming his speech in a panic.*

He couldn't stand the idea of his best friend marrying his sister. He saw you two together at tonight's engagement party and it drove him half mad and he snapped and killed Charles!

SANDRA. But if it is Thomas, what if our affair is discovered?

MAX. I have no doubt in my mind he would try and kill us as well, just like he killed Charles!

SANDRA. Oh I feel faint again!

MAX. Don't worry, Florence. Just follow my lead.

> *Chris opens the door.*

CHRIS. I'm sorry to have kept you.

> *The heraldic shield over the door swings down and hits Chris in the face. Chris hastily pulls it off the wall and throws it offstage.*

…But now I have finished examining the body our interviews can proceed. *(Calls off.)* Perkins! Bring in Charles' personal effects.

> *Dennis enters with lots of bulky personal props.*

DENNIS. Where would you like them, Inspector?

CHRIS. Set them down on the mantelpiece.

> *Chris realises what he's said.*

DENNIS. As you wish, Inspector.

*Dennis carries the props over to Annie, who is still holding the candlesticks. Dennis carefully balances the items in between the candlesticks. Dennis is supposed to leave but doesn't. Silence.*

CHRIS. Don't go, Perkins.

*Dennis goes to leave and then stops.*

I'd like to ask you a few questions first. Mr. Haversham, Miss Colleymoore, if you'd be so kind as to give us a moment's privacy.

MAX. Naturally.

*Max and Sandra exit. Dennis sits down on the chaise longue.*

CHRIS. Don't just stand there, Perkins, take a seat.

*Dennis sits down again. He takes out a cigarette case.*

DENNIS. May I?

CHRIS. Go ahead. How are you feeling, Perkins?

DENNIS. A little shaken, sir.

*Dennis takes a cigarette out of the case and then puts the case in Annie's mouth. She protests but is quickly silenced by the case.*

But I'll be fine.

CHRIS. You and Charles Haversham, you were close?

DENNIS. Yes, sir, very close.

*Dennis goes to light his cigarette; he burns his hand and drops the match into the coal scuttle, where it suddenly ignites the scotch. Annie is alarmed by the fire and disappears backstage, dropping all of the props loudly onto the floor. Dennis falls back onto the chaise longue in surprise.*

CHRIS. You don't appear very upse—

*Robert bursts in wearing a fire mask and spraying a fire extinguisher wildly. He gets Dennis more than the coal scuttle. Robert bellows, "Don't worry I've got it under control," etc. Robert realises he's been seen. He looks at the audience in silence. The extinguisher suddenly goes off again in his hand, making Robert jump slightly. Robert lifts the fire mask.*

ROBERT. *(Ad libs.)* Evening, Inspector. We require the coal in the library. *(Or similar vamp.)*

*Robert withdraws, taking the coal scuttle with him.*

DENNIS. On the contrary—

ROBERT. *(Off.)* Of course they didn't notice.

DENNIS. —I've barely—

ROBERT. *(Off.)* I improvised!

DENNIS. He was such a kindly, charming man.

CHRIS. It's true.

DENNIS. You met him?

CHRIS. Once at the local police station. He was a consultant on a fraud case I was working on.

DENNIS. I see.

CHRIS. How long have you been working at Haversham Manor?

DENNIS. Eighty years.

CHRIS. Eighty / years?

DENNIS. *(Corrects himself.)* Eight years! Eight / years.

CHRIS. Eight years. And have you enjoyed your time here?

DENNIS. My time with Mr. Haversham has been nothing but a joy. I feel that since I've come here I have been seen not only as a butler but also as a friend and a confidant. If you need me I'll be in my quarters. Exits.

> *Chris stares at him furiously.*

Exits!

> *Dennis realises and turns to go. He gathers up the props Annie dropped on the floor.*

CHRIS. *Thank you, Perkins!* If you'd be so kind as to send in Florence Colleymoore on your way out.

> *Sandra bursts in, followed by Robert. Dennis exits.*

SANDRA. No need, I'm already here. Don't ask too much of me, Inspector, I feel fragile as glass.

> *Sandra slams the door. We hear a huge crash as Dennis drops all of the props behind it.*

CHRIS. At last, Colleymoore, you managed to find me a pencil?

ROBERT. Yes…Inspector.

> *Robert holds out the keys. Pause. Chris takes them.*

CHRIS.  And my notebook?

> *Robert holds out the vase. Pause. Chris takes it.*

I knew I'd left them somewhere. I'm going to have to speak to your sister alone.

ROBERT.  Very well. I'll be in the library, Florence.

> *Robert opens the door. Dennis is knelt down in the doorway, having collected all the props. Robert walks straight into him, causing Dennis to drop them all again as Robert closes the door behind him.*

*Dennis!*

CHRIS.  Don't fret, Miss Colleymoore, my questions will be brief and to the point and then you can get some rest. Firstly, how old are you, Miss Colleymoore?

SANDRA.  Twenty-one.

CHRIS.  I'll make a note of that.

> *He tries to make a note by dragging one of the keys across the side of the vase. It clinks as it goes across the cut glass.*

And when were you engaged to be married?

SANDRA.  In the new year.

> *Chris writes on vase again.*

CHRIS.  And when did you and your fiancé first meet?

SANDRA.  Only seven months ago, but my brother has known him since school, he introduced us at a local gala and it was love at first sight. I knew from the very first moment I saw him that he was the man I wished to marry.

> *Pause.*

CHRIS.  *(Ad-libs.)* Ah, I've run out of paper.

> *Chris puts the keys into the vase and puts the vase down on the s. r. table. Sandra comes in a line too early, causing the lines to go out of sync. The two become more frantic as they try to get back on track.*

SANDRA.  When you love someone there's no such thing as rushing, Inspector.

CHRIS.  Did you ever think you were rushing into this marriage?

SANDRA. Why wouldn't I love him?

CHRIS. Did you love him, then?

SANDRA. How could anyone have benefitted?

CHRIS. Can you think of anyone who might have benefitted from your fiancé's death?

SANDRA. Cecil?

CHRIS. Not even Cecil?

SANDRA. I wasn't having an affair! Don't raise your voice to me, Inspector!

CHRIS. YOU WERE HAVING AN AFFAIR!

SANDRA. *(Slaps Chris.)* Don't tell me to calm down!

CHRIS. Calm down, Miss Colleymoore. *(Reacts to slap.)*

SANDRA. But where did you find it?

CHRIS. I found your letter; the one addressed to Cecil, written in your hand, declaring your love for him and saying that the thought of marrying Charles repulsed you.

SANDRA. Charles read it—

CHRIS. *(Does Sandra's line for her in a high voice.)* But where did you find it? *(Back to his normal voice.)* I'll tell you where I found it: in Charles' pocket!

SANDRA. Charles read it?! Then it was suicide!

CHRIS. *Indeed! (Returning to a calmer delivery.)* Or a murder, conceived by yourself and Cecil Haversham so you could run away together.

SANDRA. You diabolical beast. How can you? I won't stand for this, Inspector. Accuse me again and you'll be sorr…

> *Robert bursts in, followed by Max; the door hits Sandra sharply on the head and she collapses, unconscious. Trevor picks up a first-aid kit and heads out of his box.*

ROBERT. What's all this shouting?

MAX. What is this, Inspector?

> *Robert and Chris see that Sandra is on the floor. Max looks at Chris and doesn't see what's happened to Sandra.*

CHRIS. I'm merely interviewing Miss Colleymoore, nothing more.

MAX. What's the matter, Florence?

*Max turns to see Sandra on the floor.*

*Calm down!* Stop shouting.

*Sandra remains unconscious.*

ROBERT. She's having one of her episodes. Snap out of it, you're hysterical.

*Sandra remains unconscious.*

MAX. Florence! Where are you going?

*Sandra remains unconscious.*

ROBERT. Come back here this instant.

*Sandra remains unconscious. Robert looks back to Max and Chris.*

She's run off. I'll fetch her back. You stay here, Cecil, I daresay the Inspector has some questions for you. You were Charles' brother after all.

*Robert exits.*

MAX. I'm sorry about her, Inspector, she's badly shaken, we all are. It's been—

*Max almost walks into the pillar again but just avoids it.*

—quite the night and it's getting late.

CHRIS. Indeed. Eleven o'clock already.

*Chris looks at the clock. The hands are at five o'clock.*

MAX. Well do you have any questions for me, Inspector?

CHRIS. Yes, similar questions to those I asked Miss Colleymoore.

MAX. Fire away, Inspector, I'm at your service.

CHRIS. Indeed. You and your brother, did you get along well?

MAX. Up and down. There was rather more strain on our relationship when Father died. And it was no secret that our father cared for Charley more than myself.

CHRIS. I see. This is your father in the portrait, is it not?

*Chris turns to the portrait. It is of a dog.*

MAX. It is.

CHRIS. He was the spitting image of Charles, wasn't he?

MAX. He was ever since he was quite young, yes.

CHRIS. You were the junior by four years?

MAX. Almost four and didn't I know it.

> *Jonathan and Robert peer through the curtains to see if Sandra is alright. Then they reach through the window and drag Sandra towards them, her body slamming against the bottom of the flat.*

Charles patronised and embarrassed me throughout our entire childhood. He always thought he knew best, and Father always took his side. If he ever didn't get his way he was unbearable.

> *Sandra's body is hoisted roughly up behind the curtain and then dropped back down.*

CHRIS. He sounds far from the ideal brother. In fact it sounds like you hated one another.

> *Sandra's dress has ridden up, revealing her underwear. Robert's hand reaches down and pulls the dress back over the underwear.*

MAX. I won't lie, Inspector, Charles and I never truly saw—

> *Max turns and sees what is going on behind him as Sandra is roughly lifted and dropped again.*

—*eye to eye!* But if you're suggesting I had something to do with his murder then you're mistaken.

CHRIS. I see. It's a dark night, Cecil.

MAX. Inspector!

> *Chris pulls the curtains open, revealing Robert, Annie, Trevor and Jonathan. They all freeze and try not to be seen. Sandra is held unconscious, in an awkward position.*

CHRIS. You can barely even make out the trees.

> *Silence. Then Chris and Max turn back D.S. As Max continues with his next line, Robert, Trevor, Annie and Jonathan continue to remove Sandra, but more noisily than before. Vamp shouting at each other, yelling instructions on how best to*

*carry Sandra out. Max and Chris shout their lines over them.*

MAX.  *What are you saying, Inspector?*

CHRIS.  *I'm saying, Cecil, that tonight would be the perfect night for you to murder your brother.*

MAX.  *Inspector, please, me and my brother had our differences, but deep down we cared for one another.*

CHRIS.  AND YET YOU HAD AN AFFAIR WITH HIS FIANCÉE?

*The group in the window drop Sandra and start again.*

MAX.  WHAT ON EARTH GAVE YOU THAT IDEA?

CHRIS.  *THIS LETTER I FOUND IN CHARLES' POCKET FROM MISS COLLEYMOORE TO YOURSELF.*

MAX.  *YOU KNOW ABOUT THAT?*

CHRIS.  *I DO! AS, IT SEEMS…DID…CHARLES!!*

*The others have managed to get Sandra out of the window. Annie sharply draws the curtains.*

MAX.  Well bravo, Inspector! You've found out about Florence and I, but it proves nothing.

*Panicking, Max begins to mime his speech as he says it, building faster and faster to a climax.*

We had nothing to do with Charles' murder, but Thomas Colleymoore does. Oh Inspector, he's a dangerously unhinged man, with a devil of a temper and Florence is his sister. Now I've said it once before and I shall say it once again: He couldn't stand the idea of giving her up to any man, let alone his old school chum. He saw them together at tonight's engagement party and he lost control and he lashed out at Charles. A crime of passion perhaps, but there it is!

*Max strikes a pose.*

CHRIS.  Thank you, Mr. Haversham, you've been most helpful.

*If Max's speech gets a round of applause, Max takes a bow and vamps, bowing as many times as he can and clapping himself until Chris bellows, "Thank you, Mr. Haversham," and stops him.*

Thank you, Mr. Haversham!…you've been most helpful. Perhaps

you could fetch Thomas Colleymoore. I'm going to have to follow more than one line of enquiry at a time to get to the bottom of this.

MAX.  At once, Inspector, anything to help the progress of your investigation.

*Max exits, slamming his arm in the door.*

Argh!

*Max withdraws his arm and closes the door.*

CHRIS.  Hang it all, Charles. Who could've killed you? Everybody under this damned roof seems guilty.

*Chris sits on the chaise longue.*

That's queer. There's something underneath these cushions. A ledger?

*Chris lifts up the cushions; there is no ledger. He begins to search for it around the chaise longue. Chris vamps to cover, repeating "A ledger?" over and over, becoming more desperate. He calls offstage for the ledger, at first in fury then eventually in despair. There is sometimes a bit of audience interaction here. Often an audience member will shout, "It's underneath," or something similar, to which Chris can respond:*

"What?"

*Audience member repeats.*

"What?"

*Audience member repeats.*

"This is not a gameshow."

*Chris responds to the audience laugh.*

"Stop laughing! Stop laughing!"

*He repeats as the audience continue to laugh.*

"This is not like television, I can see you as well!"

*Chris finally sees the ledger under the chaise longue.*

Ahh! A ledger! *(Repeats the line again quietly as if he has seen the ledger for the first time.)* A ledger…with Charles' initials inscribed on the cover. Let me see. Notes, bills… what's this?

*Chris takes a folded document tied up with ribbon out of the ledger.*

A newly written last will and testament dated only today? Let me see…

> *Chris tries to untie the ribbon on the document, but he can't. He reads off of the closed document.*

"I, Charles Haversham, hereby amend my last will and testament to leave my money, possessions and Haversham Manor to one…" Good Lord!

> *Max and Robert enter. Chris hurriedly puts the will back into the ledger.*

MAX.  Inspector. Thomas Colleymoore for you.

CHRIS.  Thank you, Cecil, but before I question Mr. Colleymoore I have some papers I'd like to review in Charles' study. I shall return presently.

MAX.  Do take your time, Inspector.

ROBERT.  Indeed.

> *Chris gets into the elevator carriage and closes the doors.*

MAX.  Tell me, Thomas, did you manage to find Florence.

ROBERT.  She ran out into the grounds.

> *A dreadful clanking is heard from the elevator.*

MAX.  And what were your feelings about—

> *Chris shoves the upstairs elevator doors open to reveal the elevator has stopped halfway between the two levels. Chris climbs out onto the upper level. He slides the ledger forward out of his way, but it goes too far and slips off the edge of the upper level. Robert catches it and throws it back up to Chris.*

And what were your feelings about Charles and Florence's engagement?

> *Chris slams the elevator doors shut upstairs, causing the downstairs voice pipe funnel to fall off the wall. Robert picks up the funnel and puts it back on the wall. This causes the barometer to fall off. As the action continues downstairs, Chris moves the chair D.S. on the upper level. He sits down and starts to examine the will.*

ROBERT.  I was overjoyed of course. I love Florence and I loved Charles, I couldn't have approved more of the match.

> *Max picks up the barometer and puts it back on the wall, causing the painting of the dog to fall down. Max catches the painting, leaving the barometer to Robert. They are left holding all three items up.*

MAX. Come now, Colleymoore, it's well known that you're over-protective of your sister.

> *Just as Max gets the painting up into position, the telephone rings. They look to it, unsure of how they will answer it.*

I'll get it.

> *Max tries hard to keep holding the picture against the wall and reach for the phone. The phone keeps ringing; finally he tries to hook it with his foot. The receiver falls off of the telephone and further away on the floor.*

Good evening.

> *Beat.*

It's for you.

ROBERT. Who the devil is it?

MAX. Your accountants, Colleymoore.

ROBERT. At half past eleven in the evening?

MAX. Yes.

ROBERT. Then hand me the receiver, Cecil.

> *Max slides the receiver in between his feet and manages to throw it up with his feet and catch it in his free hand. Vamp with the audience here if they respond. Max can show off by throwing it up again and catching it, then repeating and dropping it even further away than it was before and having to pick it up again. Max stretches and passes the receiver to Robert, who puts it to his ear, keeping the voice pipe in place with his foot and the barometer on the wall using his head.*

(*In extreme discomfort.*) Good evening. Yes, Thomas Colleymoore speaking. It is inconvenient, yes!… My recent deposits? What of them?… Discrepancies? What are you talking about, man?… Gone? Gone where?… Nine thousand pounds stolen? Good God, man! Perkins, get in here.

> *Dennis enters through the door as far as he can, knocking*

*Robert down to his knees, struggling to keep everything in place.*

DENNIS. Yes, sir.

ROBERT. Bring me my bankbook, Perkins.

*Dennis produces the bankbook.*

DENNIS. Your bankbook, sir.

*Dennis puts the bankbook into Robert's mouth.*

ROBERT. *(Muffled by the book.)* Thank you, Perkins.

DENNIS. Your pen, sir.

*Dennis produces a pen and forces it into Robert's mouth as well.*

ROBERT. *(Even more muffled.)* Thank you, Perkins.

*Robert rearranges himself to take the phone again.*

This is an absolute disgrace! Who am I speaking with? I'll report you to your superiors. Mr. Fitzroy. I'll write that name down.

*Robert writes "Mr. Fitzroy" in the bankbook with a lot of difficulty.*

Mr... Fi...tz...roy...ro...ro...ro...oy, I'll have you know this telephone call has put me in a very difficult position. Now look here, Fitzroy, I didn't authorise this transaction, but you find out who did and you call me back.

*Robert throws the phone to Max, who hangs it up.*

MAX. What is it, Colleymoore?

ROBERT. Nine thousand pounds taken from my private savings.

MAX. Good Lord!

ROBERT. What a ghastly evening.

MAX. Thomas, I'm afraid I have a confession to make.

ROBERT. Mm?

MAX. Well... Florence and I are having an affair!

ROBERT. WHAT?!

*Robert launches himself at Max, who dives D.S. The dog picture, funnel and barometer mysteriously all stay hung in their positions. Robert and Max double-take.*

You and my sister?!

*Robert throws Max s. l.*

MAX.  Now calm down, Colleymoore.

ROBERT.  You always were a snake in the grass, Cecil.

*Robert throws Max d.s.*

MAX.  It's not what you think! We're in love!

*Robert pulls Max up by his hair and drags him back up around the chaise longue, accidentally slamming his head into the side of the clock. Robert draws a sword from the fireplace.*

ROBERT.  My sister does not love you. How dare you lay a finger on her? Your own brother's fiancée; it's disgusting.

*Robert slickly thrusts his sword upwards, removing and catching the scabbard.*

No wonder your father hated you.

MAX.  Don't speak about my father, Colleymoore!

*Max copies Robert's move, but the scabbard does not fly off the sword, it comes off a bit and slides back down. Max pulls off the scabbard instead and draws his sword.*

ROBERT.  The time has come for you to answer to me for your indiscretions. Draw your swo…

*Robert turns to see Max's sword is already drawn.*

En garde!

*They fight a few slick choreographed moves.*

Nice try, Cecil, but no match for my skill. You know sometimes I forget you're Charley's brother, you're so pathetic.

*They fight again. Max leaps off of the back of the chaise longue.*

MAX.  I always was *too—*

*Max narrowly misses the pillar again.*

—quick for you, but still not bad, Colleymoore.

*Max stamps on the floor, causing a floorboard to flip up and hit him in the face. Max looks fine for a moment but then collapses out of sight behind the chaise longue. Max starts to get back to his feet. We hear a metallic snapping sound. Max slowly pulls his sword up from behind the chaise, revealing that it's broken (now just a handle and a short stump of blade). Max makes sword clanging sound effects as they continue fighting.*

Ching! Ching! Ching!

ROBERT. Rattle! Clang!

MAX. Ching!

ROBERT. Swipe!

MAX. Slice!

ROBERT. Ah, 'tis nothing.

MAX. Have at you, Colleymoore! Ching! Ching! Ching!

*Max beats Robert to the floor s. L. below the upper level and does two victory swipes as he walks away.*

Yes! Swipe Swipe! You've got a good parry, Colleymoore.

ROBERT. Good parry? I'll show you a good parry!

*Robert springs to his feet, accidentally thrusting his sword through the underside of the upper level. The blade goes straight through and comes up between Chris' legs, narrowly missing his crotch. Robert tries to pull his sword back but finds it stuck. Robert continues the fight without his sword.*

I'll show you a good parry!

MAX and ROBERT. Ching! Ching!

ROBERT. Slash!

MAX. Disarm!

*Max throws his broken piece of sword into the fireplace.*

ROBERT. Slash!

*Max pulls a red strip of fabric blood out of a hole in his jumper.*

MAX. Blood! Aaaah!

*Max vamps with the audience, miming and doing the sounds of the blood squirting and then pouring from his wound.*

ROBERT. I don't need this to kill a man like you, Haversham!

*Robert throws Max to the floor.*

41

It seems there's no mystery as to who killed Charles anymore.

> *Robert drags Max to the door. He swings it open, banging Max in the head as he does so, and then throws Max out of the room.*

He was killed by his own vile little brother in a fit of jealous rage. You'll be sorry you ever laid a finger on my sister, Haversham. You'll be sorry!

> *Robert exits, slamming the door. The dog picture, voice pipe funnels, barometer, window grille, curtains and curtain rails all crash down off of the wall. Dennis is revealed in the window with a glass of sherry on a tray. He runs in through the door and puts the tray down by the telephone. Three loud gunshots and Max screaming are heard offstage.*

DENNIS. Gunshots in the library!

CHRIS. *(Picking up the voice pipe funnel and speaking into it.)* Dear God, what's going on down there?

DENNIS. *(Picking up the barometer downstairs and speaking into it.)* I don't know, Inspector. I heard gunshots. Please come down here.

CHRIS. *(Into the pipe.)* I'm on my way, Perkins.

> *Chris gets in the elevator and it begins to descend. Robert enters through the downstairs door.*

ROBERT. Inspector! Inspector! Where's Inspector Carter?

DENNIS. He's coming down now in the elevator, Mr. Colleymoore.

> *We hear the elevator crash to the floor. Chris bursts out of it in a cloud of smoke, looking shaken.*

ROBERT. There you are, Inspector. I don't know how you manage to look so calm and collected in a situation such as this.

CHRIS. It comes from years of experience.

ROBERT. Indeed.

CHRIS. It is important we remain calm and we don't let each other out of our sight. Where's Miss Colleymoore?

ROBERT. She's coming now. Get in here, Florence.

> *Jonathan opens the downstairs door and pushes Annie onstage.*

*Annie is wearing Sandra's dress over her own clothes and clutches a script.*

Florence, you don't look yourself this evening.

ANNIE. *(Reading each word slowly from her script in an American accent.)* Thomas, I'm frightened.

ROBERT. Don't worry, Florence; you're safe in here with me.

DENNIS. What's happening, sir?

CHRIS. Isn't it obvious? Cecil has lost control.

ANNIE. Oh no not Cecil. *(Pronounced "ke-sill.")*

CHRIS. He killed Charles tonight, driven mad by his lust for you and now he knows we've found him out.

ANNIE. I cannot bear it. Cecil *(Again pronounced "ke-sill.")* would not do such a thing.

DENNIS. Well this is a fine mess. The worst night I've seen in eighty— *(Corrects himself.)* eight years of service.

ANNIE. Save me, brother.

*Annie goes to Chris, who pushes her back to Robert.*

Ooh, save me, brother.

ROBERT. Don't worry, Florence. I shan't let anyone hurt a hair on your head.

ANNIE. I'm panicking.

*Annie does a physical action to show she is panicking.*

I can't believe…Cecil— *(Still pronounced "ke-sill.")*

CHRIS. *Cecil!*

ANNIE. Cecil…is doing this.

DENNIS. Try to relax, Miss Colleymoore.

ANNIE. I shall faint.

ROBERT. You shan't faint—

*Annie falls back without warning. Robert just catches her.*

—confound it! What a devil of a situation this is. Now—

*Jonathan bursts in, holding his gun.*

JONATHAN. Not so fast, Insp… *(Realises.)* oh for God's sake!

*Jonathan realises he is still too early and exits.*

ROBERT. Now we're—

> *Jonathan walks past the window, his head in his hand. He slowly realises the audience can see him. Mortified, he lowers himself out of view.*

Now we're all going to survive tonight, you hear me?

> *Chris peers out of the door.*

CHRIS. Take cover!

ROBERT. Great Scott!

DENNIS. Good heavens!

ANNIE. Ay me!

CHRIS. Don't panic, Cecil is crossing the landing. We must lock him out!

ROBERT. Quickly, where are the keys to the door, Perkins?

DENNIS. Here they are, sir.

> *Dennis pulls out the Inspector's notebook from his pocket. Chris upends the vase, sending the keys flying across the stage. Dennis drops the notebook and catches the keys.*

Here they are, sir.

CHRIS. Hand them to me quickly, Perkins, before Cecil bursts in—

> *The door bursts open and Max staggers inside.*

DENNIS and ROBERT. No! No!

> *Max shuffles forward a few paces and then flops dead onto the chaise longue. We see three bullet wounds in his back.*

Good Lord!

> *Lights shift to red and the short musical spike plays. Then the lights shift back.*

ANNIE. Cecil's dead?

> *Lights shift to red again. The same short musical spike plays. The lights shift back.*

DENNIS. A double murder!

> *The lights turn to red and a short burst of an English new*

*wave song like "Girls on Film" by Duran Duran plays.** Then the correct musical spike cuts in. The lights shift back.*

TREVOR.  Found the Duran Duran.****

CHRIS.  Time of death: quarter to mid…

*Chris looks at the clock. It still reads five o'clock.*

Five o'clock.

ANNIE.  Cecil! No. No. No. I loved him. I loved him. I know it was wrong. I know I was engaged to Charles.

*She makes a noise of realisation—Annie was unaware of this bit of the story.*

—but Cecil was mine and.

*Silence. Chris turns the page in her script.*

…I was his.

DENNIS.  There there, Miss Colleymoore.

ANNIE.  How will I go on? Sobs.

CHRIS.  You! Take this body outside.

DENNIS.  Yes, Inspector.

ROBERT.  I'll lend you a hand, Perkins.

*Dennis exits.*

CHRIS.  I've seen an awful lot in the twenty years I've been an Inspector.

*Dennis reenters, carrying the two stretcher poles from earlier. Dennis and Robert lay them on the floor in front of the chaise longue and roll Max on top of them.*

But two murders on one evening is certainly unusual.

*Robert and Dennis lift the poles. Max grasps them and holds on for dear life. Robert and Dennis carry Max to the door. Robert and Dennis can't get Max off through the door, so they rotate him ninety degrees onto his side and exit through the door. Annie shuts the door behind them.*

*Robert backs up past the window, revealing Max still on the*

---

* See Note on Songs/Recordings at the back of this volume.

** If a song by a different band is used, change "Duran Duran" appropriately.

*poles. Max grins at the audience; Robert and Dennis quickly lower him out of view. Max stands up in the window and grins at the audience again. Robert grabs him and pulls him out of sight; Max smacks his head on the edge of the window as he goes.*

ANNIE. Oh Inspector, my fiancé and my lover killed on the same eve.

CHRIS. Remember your breathing, Miss Colleymoore, now is not the time for another of your episodes.

ANNIE. *(Calm.)* I am having an episode, Inspector. I cannot help it.

CHRIS. *(Under his breath.)* Have an episode. Have…an…episode. *(Loudly.)* Have an episode.

> *Annie tries to scream and shake as she has seen Sandra do in rehearsals. Vamp. Annie builds the episode bigger and bigger until it reaches a climax and she flops onto the chaise longue.*

No, Miss Colleymoore.

> *Robert and Dennis reenter.*

ROBERT. Florence, control yourself girl.

DENNIS. She's having another one of her hysterical episodes.

ANNIE. *(Calmly reads.)* They're dead. They're gone and they're never coming back.

ROBERT. I will not tolerate another tantrum, Florence.

ANNIE. *(Calm.)* Get away from me, Thomas. You don't understand my grief.

ROBERT. That's enough, take one of your pills.

ANNIE. No. Not more pills.

> *Annie takes a pill with no hesitation.*

Oh, they're mints.

ROBERT. But who could have killed…

> *Annie upstages Robert by sinking back onto the chaise longue, pretending to be knocked out by the pill.*

But who could have killed him?

DENNIS. That's a good question, Mr. Colleymoore.

CHRIS. …and one we need to answer quickly if we're going to get out of this house alive.

ANNIE. Oh Inspector, you've given me a chill.

CHRIS. Perkins, pour us all another scotch.

DENNIS. Of course, Inspector.

*Dennis pours more white spirit for everyone.*

CHRIS. Now, tell me, is there anyone else that you know of in the grounds other than the four of us?

ANNIE. Not a soul.

ROBERT. The gardener left at six, the only other member of staff is Perkins. *(Drinks and spits out the white spirit.)* Good God, I needed that.

CHRIS. Does anyone have access to the grounds?

ANNIE. No one, Inspector.

DENNIS. I'm the only one with a master key and as instructed I locked and bolted the doors as soon as you arrived.

ROBERT. Then who could have killed him?

DENNIS. That's a good question, Mr. Colleymoore.

CHRIS. …and one we need to answer quickly if we're going to get out of this house alive.

ANNIE. Oh Inspector, you've given me a chill.

CHRIS. Perkins, pour us all another scotch.

*Chris and Robert start to realise that they have been here before.*

DENNIS. Of course, Inspector.

*Dennis pours white spirit again.*

CHRIS. Now, tell me, is there anyone else that you know of in the grounds other than the four of us?

ANNIE. Not a soul.

ROBERT. The gardener left at six, the only other member of staff is Perkins. *(Drinks. Spits it out again.)* Good God, I needed that.

CHRIS. Does anyone have access to the grounds?

ANNIE. No one, Inspector.

DENNIS. I'm the only one with a master key and as instructed I locked and bolted the doors as soon as you arrived.

ROBERT. *(Pointedly, hoping Dennis will say the correct line this time.)* Then who could have killed him?

> *Dennis knows something is wrong but not what, and the loop of dialogue goes around again.*

DENNIS. That's a good question, Mr. Colleymoore.

CHRIS. …and one we need to answer quickly if we're going to get out of this house alive.

ANNIE. Oh Inspector, you've given me a chill.

CHRIS. Perkins, pour us all another scotch.

DENNIS. Of course, Inspector.

> *Dennis pours white spirit again.*

CHRIS. Now, tell me, is there anyone else that you know of in the grounds other than the four of us?

ANNIE. Not a soul.

ROBERT. The gardener left at six, the only other member of staff is Perkins. *(Drinks. Spits.)* Good God, I needed that.

CHRIS. Does anyone have access to the grounds?

ANNIE. No one, Inspector.

DENNIS. I'm the only one with the master key and as instructed I locked and bolted all the doors as soon as you arrived.

ROBERT. *Then who could have killed him?*

> *Pause. All look at Dennis.*

DENNIS. That's a good question, Mr. Colleymoore.

> *The script loops again. Much faster this time.*

CHRIS. …and one we need to answer quickly if we're going to get out of this house alive.

ANNIE. Oh Inspector, you've given me a chill!

CHRIS. Perkins, pour us all another scotch.

DENNIS. Of course, Inspector.

> *Dennis pours white spirit again.*

CHRIS. Now, tell me, is there anyone else that you know of in the grounds other than the four of us?

ANNIE. Not a soul.

ROBERT. The gardener left at six, the only other member of staff is Perkins. *(Drinks again. Spits out again.)* Good God, I needed that.

CHRIS. Does anyone have access to the grounds?

ANNIE. No one, Inspector.

DENNIS. I'm the only one with a master key and as instructed I locked and bolted the doors as soon as you arrived.

ROBERT. *THEN WHO COULD HAVE KILLED HIM?*

> *Pause. Tense, everyone desperate that Dennis will get it right this time.*

DENNIS. That's a good question, Mr. Colleymoore.

ROBERT and CHRIS. *Argh!!*

CHRIS. …and one we need to answer quickly if we're going to get out of this house alive.

ANNIE. Oh Inspector, you've given me a chill.

CHRIS. Perkins, pour us all another scotch.

DENNIS. Of course, Inspector.

> *Dennis pours white spirit again.*

CHRIS. Now, tell me, is there anyone else that you know of in the grounds other than the four of us?

ANNIE. Not a soul.

ROBERT. The gardener left at six, the only other member of staff is Perkins. *(Throws the white spirit in Dennis' face.)* Good God, I needed that!

> *Chris throws his white spirit in Dennis' face as well.*

CHRIS. Does anyone have access to the grounds?

ANNIE. No one, Inspector.

DENNIS. *(In pain, the white spirit burning his skin.)* I'm the only one with a master key and as instructed I locked and bolted all the doors as soon as you arrived.

> *Chris and Robert grab Dennis.*

ALL. Then who could have killed him?

DENNIS. *(Realises.)* No one! YES! No one could have killed him, except for the people who are in this room.

CHRIS. Good God, you're right, it's one of us.

*All gasp.*

ANNIE. *(Reads.)* This is a disaster! Blackout. Intermission.

*Annie realises her mistake.*

Oh.

*Blackout. Tabs fly in. Music.*

## End of Act One

*INTERVAL ACTIVITY:*

*Robert appears in auditorium/foyer in a robe and joins the queue for ice creams. Chris appears and sends him backstage.*

# ACT TWO

*Dramatic house music plays.*

*The house lights fade; shouting is heard behind the tabs. Chris emerges from under the tabs. A spotlight comes up on him.*

CHRIS. Good evening again, ladies and gentlemen, I hope you have enjoyed the break, we will be resuming this evening's performance momentarily I am assured. I… I must say I'm delighted to see that so many of you have returned for the second act.

Obviously I would be lying if I said the first act went entirely as rehearsed, there were one or two minor snags, which you may or may not have picked up on. But they are snags that you would expect to see in any production. And this certainly hasn't been the worst first act Cornley Drama Society has seen by some stretch.

*Chris gives a hollow laugh.*

Just last year due to a casting error Cornley Drama Society had to present *Snow White and the Seven Tall Broad Gentlemen.* Anyway—

*Chris is interrupted by Trevor's voice over his radio.*

TREVOR. *(Over radio.)* …No, it's going quite badly to be honest, buddy.

CHRIS. Before we begin again—

TREVOR. *(Over radio.)* Yeah, she's still unconscious and we still can't find the dog—

CHRIS. Trevor!

Before we resume the production, one word of health and safety administration: Could I please ask anyone who consumed any of the salted nuts available during the intermission to please seek medical help immediately.

And now I present to you the concluding act of *The Murder at Haversham Manor.*

*Chris exits S. R. Spotlight out. Music. The tabs fly out, revealing chaos as Annie, Max, Robert, Dennis, Jonathan and the stage*

51

*crew all rehang the picture, voice pipe funnels, barometer, curtains, etc. They see the audience. Chris enters from the S. R. wing. He gestures offstage and the house tabs fly back in.*

*Beat. The house tabs fly back out, revealing Robert, Dennis, Chris and Annie in their positions from the end of Act One. Jonathan, Max and the stage crew have gone. All wall hangings are back in position. Beat.*

DENNIS. No one could—

*All wall hangings crash down to the floor. The cast clear everything into the wings.*

No one could have killed him, except for the people who are in this room.

CHRIS. Good God, you're right, it's one of us!

*All gasp.*

ANNIE. *(Reads from her script.)* This is a disaster.

ROBERT. And it's not over yet! Two murders on one night at Haversham Manor, what a grizzly evening.

ANNIE. Frightful, brother, frightful.

DENNIS. And look, Mr. Colleymoore, the snowstorm outside is building.

*Max appears in the window and throws snow out.*

ROBERT. If we're not careful we'll be snowed into this slaughterhouse. We must discover the guilty man.

CHRIS. Indeed. The gunshots were heard coming from the library. I shall investigate the room. All of you remain here.

*Chris exits through the downstairs door. As he opens it, Jonathan is revealed standing in the doorway ready to go on. He swiftly moves out of view.*

ROBERT. This whole business is a disgrace. Now let us remind ourselves of what we know.

DENNIS. We know that Charles Haversham was found murdered here, in his own private rooms, on the night of his engagement party.

ROBERT. We know that his fiancée was involved in an affair with his own brother, Cecil. How could my sister behave in such a way?

ANNIE. Not now, Thomas. We know that he too was murdered on the same eve, in cold blood.

DENNIS. The only thing we don't know is who the murderer is.

ANNIE. Oh, the tension in this house is…

> *Annie trips up over the rug and drops her script on the floor. The pages of her script go everywhere. Annie tries to pick up the papers, but they are all out of order.*

Oh, the tension in this house is… Oh, the tension in thi… oh it… oh, it's tense.

ROBERT. Florence. How do you feel now?

ANNIE. *(Ad libs, brightly.)* I'm good.

ROBERT. That's dreadful.

ANNIE. *(Ad libs.)* Oh dreadful, yes, I want to die!

ROBERT. That's the spirit, Florence.

DENNIS. But now, Miss Colleymoore, I must ask you an important question. Where were you when the murder was committed?

> *Dennis mimes the line to her. He points down and mimes drinking a cup of tea. Annie misinterprets.*

ANNIE. On the floor with a moustache.

ROBERT. That makes perfect sense. So was I.

> *Annie reads off the wrong page of the script.*

ANNIE. Kiss me a thousand times, I'm yours!

ROBERT. Of course, Florence, that's what brothers are for.

DENNIS. This is a disaster! And already it's midnight.

> *Trevor plays a loud clock chime twelve times.*

That was most—

> *Trevor hits the chime again. He sees he has confused Dennis and stops.*

…that was most—

> *Trevor hits the chime again and laughs to himself.*

TREVOR. *(To Dennis.)* Sorry, buddy, go on.

DENNIS. That w—

*Trevor hits the chime again. Chris opens the study door.*

CHRIS. *Trevor!*

*Chris closes the study door.*

DENNIS. That was most ominous. *(Pronounced "omoo-noose.")*

ROBERT. Ominous indeed.

*Chris enters upstairs, holding a gun. He calls into the voice pipe.*

CHRIS. Study to lounge. Are you there, Colleymoore?

ROBERT. *(Calling up to Chris.)* Yes, Inspector.

CHRIS. Colleymoore, come up to the study quickly. I must speak with you.

ROBERT. At once, Inspector.

*Robert gets into the elevator carriage. We hear the elevator breaking. He falls out in a cloud of smoke.*

CHRIS. There you are, Colleymoore!

ROBERT. Yes, Inspector.

*Robert tries to climb up to the upper level.*

CHRIS. I must speak with you, Thomas.

ROBERT. Of course, Carter.

CHRIS. Are you sitting comfortably?

ROBERT. Most comfortably, Inspector.

*Dennis and Annie try to push Robert up.*

CHRIS. Before we speak, I must check no one else is in earshot.

ROBERT. No one else is here, Inspector.

CHRIS. Very well. Colleymoore, I have found the weapon that was used to kill Cecil Haversham.

*Robert manages to get up onto the upper level and takes the gun from Chris.*

ROBERT. Good Lord, where was it?

CHRIS. In the library, lying on the table. Muzzle warm and the barrel still smoking.

ROBERT. Someone killed Cecil with this?

CHRIS. Yes, less than half an hour ago.

ROBERT. But who?

CHRIS. I was hoping you would be able to tell me that, Colleymoore. After all we are friends, aren't we?

ROBERT. I have no idea who killed Cecil, I was down in the kitchens when I heard the gunshots, fetching my sister some refreshment…

> *Robert forgets his line.*

Line!

TREVOR. *(On his way out of his tech box.)* I don't know what page we're on, buddy!

ROBERT. I don't know what page we're on, buddy.

> *Robert realises this isn't the line and looks to Trevor furiously.*

CHRIS. *(Prompts Robert.)* Besides why would I / want to…

ROBERT. Besides why would I want to kill my oldest friend's younger brother?

CHRIS. Perhaps because you found out about his affair with Florence. We all know you're a jealous man, Colleymoore; ruthlessly protective of your sister.

ROBERT. Protective! I approve of whatever makes my sister happy.

CHRIS. Don't play the fool with me, Thomas. You shot Cecil Haversham in cold blood and you know that wasn't the plan.

> *Chris and Robert pose with their hands on their chins. Lights shift to downstairs. There is a heavy knock at the door.*

DENNIS. Who the devil could that be?

ANNIE. *(Searches through the pages.)* Err… I don't know!

DENNIS. You're probably right! Quickly, Miss Colleymoore, we must hide you out of harm's way. Charles had a secret passage built behind this bookcase. Stand back, I'll open it.

> *Dennis pulls a book down from the bookshelf. Nothing happens. Dennis looks at the bookcase. It turns and swallows Dennis up.*

*(Off.)* Step inside, Miss Colleymoore.

> *Annie steps in front of the bookcase, and it swivels again, swallowing her and spitting Dennis back out. Dennis goes around again. Annie follows around after him.*

You're safe in there—

> *As Dennis reemerges, this time Trevor is spat out after him. More knocking comes from the downstairs door. Trevor goes to exit through the door but hears more knocking, panics and hides in the grandfather clock.*

You're safe in there, Miss Colleymoore.

> *Dennis opens the downstairs door. Thunder and lightning. Max stands in the doorway dressed as a new character (Arthur the Gardener) in an overcoat, with mutton chops, a watering can and holding a lead with no dog. Max gives the same performance he did as Cecil.*

Arthur the Gardener! What are you doing here?

MAX. I was gardening late in the grounds this evening with Winston *(Holds up the lead.)* when we got caught in the storm and couldn't make it to the gates.

DENNIS. Good heavens, Arthur, come inside. You won't believe what a nightmare this evening has been.

MAX. How do you mean? Woah, Winston, down from the chaise longue!

> *He mimes holding down the invisible dog. Vamp. Max holds the imaginary dog back from going into the audience.*

DENNIS. Mr. Haversham was murdered tonight.

MAX. Mr. Haversham? Surely you don't mean Charles Haversham?

> *Max walks straight into the pillar supporting the upper level and knocks it over, causing the upper level, with Robert and Chris on it, to tip forward on an incline, still suspended. The drinks cabinet and chair slide across the floor. Chris and Robert grab them before they roll off the edge. Chris and Robert move to the door and try to go through it, but the door handle comes off in Robert's hand. They are trapped.*
>
> *Vamp. Brief inaudible argument between them. Robert tries to reattach the handle. Then suddenly together they stare out and freeze in the pose from earlier with their right hands on their chins.*

DENNIS. And not only that, his brother Cecil was also killed tonight.

MAX. Yes, well that explains the strange goings-on I have seen in the grounds this evening.

> *Max picks up the loose pillar and passes it out of the window. Jonathan is briefly seen taking it from him.*

DENNIS. Strange goings-on?

MAX. A mysterious figure stood by the window to this very room and I noticed that the latch on the window was forced and Winston found this on the ground beneath it.

> *Max produces a handkerchief from his pocket and passes it to Dennis.*

A lace handkerchief. With a deep red mark with a distinctive scent.

> *Dennis smells the handkerchief then reads off his hand.*

DENNIS. Cyanide. *(Pronounced "ky-a-nid-ee.")*

MAX. Precisely! Cyanide.

> *Dennis becomes upset he has made yet another mistake and turns u.s. to hide his emotion. Max briefly comforts Dennis, and he turns back to the audience.*

—and you can tell from the shape of the mark it's been used to hold a bottle.

> *Dennis reveals that a bottle has been crudely drawn onto the handkerchief.*

But not only that, it's embroidered with the initials F.C.

DENNIS. Florence Colleymoore.

MAX. Indeed.

> *Lights shift upstairs. Robert stops trying to reattach the door handle and puts it into the drinks cabinet.*

CHRIS. I must show you something, Thomas. No doubt you'll find it interesting.

> *Robert tries to lean against the desk and slips forward slightly.*

ROBERT. Well… *well*… well… What is it, Inspector?

CHRIS. A new draft of Charles' last will and testament, dated only tod-*ay!*

> *Chris moves and the whole upper level wobbles.*

It appears he has changed the beneficiary.

> *Chris passes the will to Robert, who cannot untie the ribbon.*

ROBERT. Who on earth has he changed the benefic… well who… on earth has he changed the beni… Well who has he—

> *Robert pretends to read off of the front of it.*

Good Lord!

CHRIS. That's right!

ROBERT. He's leaving it all to Perkins!

> *Lights shift downstairs.*

DENNIS. Arthur the Gardener, you're suggesting that Florence Colleymoore broke into Charles' private rooms this afternoon?

MAX. Florence has murdered her own fiancé!

DENNIS. Miss Colleymoore, get in here now!

> *The bookcase spins around, revealing Annie holding a new script.*

You killed Charles Haversham and we have the evidence to prove it.

ANNIE. *(Grinning, knowing she now has the correct script.)* How dare you, Perki…

> *The drinks cabinet on the upper level slips and falls towards Annie. Robert catches it. Lights shift upstairs.*

CHRIS. The time has come to confront Perkins and tell him we know what he has done! Get in the elevator, Colley…moore.

ROBERT. Yes, Inspector.

> *Robert edges over to the elevator and looks inside. He looks at Chris and shakes his head.*

CHRIS. *(Ad libs.)* Then we'll have to take the stairs.

ROBERT. *(Ad libs.)* After you.

> *Chris passes the chair to Robert, who remains frozen on the upper level. Chris slowly slides his legs off the edge of the upper level until the point of no return, when he drops down onto the lower level and stands up.*

CHRIS. Perkins.

ANNIE. *(Reading from script.)* Thank heavens, Inspector. These two have been accusing me of the most dreadful things.

MAX. Hold your tongue. We all know what you've done! Woah, Winston! Down, boy!

> *Max mimes holding the dog back from Chris.*

DENNIS. Winston, the Inspector's here to help us.

MAX. I'm sorry about Winston, Inspector. I'll put him outside.

> *Max throws the lead out through the door.*

CHRIS. Arthur, I presume?

MAX. I'm the longest serving member of staff here at Haversham Manor.

DENNIS. He's been working for Mr. Haversham for ninety years.

CHRIS. *(Aside to Dennis.)* Nine.

DENNIS. Ninety-nine years.

CHRIS. Ninety-nine years? What a dedicated man.

> *Hearing this, Max hunches over and acts as though he is incredibly old. Chris continues his line through gritted teeth.*

But Arthur, I was informed—

> *Chris turns and sees Max.*

I was informed that you left Haversham Manor at six o'clock today?

MAX. *(Old man voice.)* What's that, young man?

> *Chris grabs Max and pulls him up to standing. Max reverts to his normal performance.*

CHRIS. It would appear you were hiding in the grounds on the night two men were murdered here!

DENNIS. Arthur became trapped in the storm and couldn't make it to the gates.

CHRIS. How implausible. I don't suppose you realise what you have walked into this evening then, Arthur?

MAX. On the contrary, Inspector. It appears I have discovered a clue that will close this case.

> *Max holds out the handkerchief.*

CHRIS. A handkerchief?

DENNIS. Monogrammed. *(Pronounced "mon-oh-gram-ed.")*

CHRIS. Monogrammed.

MAX. And stained with cyanide. *(Pronounced "ky-a-nid-ee.")*

CHRIS. *Cyanide!*

MAX. Dropped beneath the forced window that was used to gain access to this room so someone could poison Charles.

CHRIS. Good God, how dreadful! I must inspect this handkerchief in more detail. Thomas, fetch my magnifying glass from Charles' desk.

ROBERT. *(Still on the upper level.)* Without delay, Inspector.

> *Robert reaches for the desk. He pulls the desk towards him and the upper level suddenly drops again, sending the desk, drinks cabinet and chair sliding down into a pile on top of him. Robert's hand emerges, rummages in the drawer and produces the magnifying glass. Robert passes the magnifying glass to Chris.*

Your magnifying glass, Inspector.

CHRIS. Thank you, Thomas.

> *The pot plant tips over, falls on top of the furniture pile.*

DENNIS. But Inspector, there is something you do not know about that handkerchie—

> *The telephone rings loudly.*

MAX. I'll get it. *(Picks up receiver.)* Good evening?… Ah yes. It's for you, Mr. Colleymoore.

ROBERT. *(From beneath the furniture.)* Another telephone call?

MAX. Yes, sir.

ROBERT. Who is it, Arthur?

MAX. Mr. Fitzroy, sir.

ROBERT. Hand me the receiver, Arthur.

MAX. At once, sir.

> *Max tries to pass Robert the receiver, but the cord doesn't reach. Annie, Max and Chris create a chain of arms from*

*the phone with Chris' hand in a phone shape at the end. When they are all at full stretch, Max releases some of his gardener's glove to give them the extra few inches they need to get the receiver to Robert's ear.*

Fitzroy! Thank you for calling again… Yes this is a much more convenient time, thank you… Another transaction traced… A one-way ticket to Dover? No I have no idea!

*Max drops his end of the gardener's glove.*

Hello? Fitzroy? Are you there?

*Chris flicks the glove and Max catches it again.*

Ah, there you are, Fitzroy. You've given nine thousand pounds of my money to someone else. You are causing me more pain than you could possibly imagine! I shall hang up the phone immediately.

*The phone is hung up.*

DENNIS. Mr. Colleymoore, you look like you could use a scotch.

ROBERT. *No!* No more scotch thank you, Perkins. What a dreadful evening! I must check my bank records once more, if you'll excuse me…

*Robert begins to try and exit through the upstairs door, crawling with all the furniture towards it.*

If you'll excuse me… *if you'll excuse me!*

*Throughout the following, Robert is very noisily trying to get off and take all the furniture with him. The upstairs door opens and Jonathan is briefly seen on the other side holding some tools. The other actors shout to cover the noise Robert is making.*

DENNIS. Inspector! There is something about the handkerchief you have not detected!

CHRIS. What is it, Perkins?

DENNIS. That handkerchief bears upon it the initials F.C.

MAX. Florence Colleymoore is the murderer, Inspector!

ANNIE. Me? The murderer? How can you?

CHRIS. You are the murderer, Miss Colleymoore. It is plain for us all to see. You were engaged to be married to Charles, a man who

61

according to your letter you despised. Not only this but you were having an affair with his brother. It seems plausible to me that you both murdered him so you could be together.

> *Robert eventually gets all the furniture out the door. More vamp or less of Chris' speech if necessary. The last item is the globe, which almost slips out of Robert's control and slides towards the edge of the upper level. Robert grabs it and throws it through the door.*

ROBERT. If you'll excuse me.

> *Robert exits and slams the door shut behind him.*

(*Off.*) I think it's going rather *WELL!*

> *Robert is immediately seen falling past the window.*

MAX. Florence Colleymoore is the murderer, Inspector!

ANNIE. Me, the murderer? How can yo—

> *Robert enters sharply through the downstairs door, knocking Annie out.*

ROBERT. I checked my bank recor...*oh!!*

CHRIS. You're lying, Florence, you killed him!

ROBERT. She's having another one of her hysterical episodes.

> *Robert and Chris lift Annie's body up and sit her on the windowsill.*

CHRIS. You killed your fiancé, Florence. What do you have to say for yourself?

> *Chris lifts Annie's face so she looks out to the audience.*

SANDRA. (*Off.*) I am no murderer!

> *Sandra bursts in through the swivel bookcase in her underwear. Chris and Robert drop Annie backwards through the window.*

CHRIS. We all know that's not true.

SANDRA. It is true, Inspector!

MAX. You've been exposed.

CHRIS. Very well, Miss Colleymoore, your name can easily be cleared. We must examine Charles' body for evidence of cyanide poisoning. Colleymoore, Perkins, show me to the service quarters so I can check the deceased once more.

DENNIS. Inspector.

CHRIS. Arthur, you stay here with Miss Colleymoore and ensure she does not leave this room.

> *Chris, Robert and Dennis exit through the downstairs door. Sandra and Max are alone again. Max stares at the floor; he cannot look at Sandra.*

SANDRA. Arthur, you have known me years, surely you believe I would never do something like this?

MAX. On the contrary, Miss Colleymoore, it was I who discovered you to be the guilty party.

SANDRA. Oh Arthur! How can you? Please, you must protect me from these fiends! I'll do anything to win your trust.

> *Sandra throws herself into Max's arms.*

MAX. Miss Colleymoore, you know I cannot resist your feminine charms.

SANDRA. I have seen the way you look at me across the grounds. Even now, the way you're looking at me.

> *Max stares away from her.*

Even now, the way you're looking at me... Even now the way you're looking at me!

> *Sandra turns Max's head to look at her.*

I know how you feel.

MAX. Please, Miss Colleymoore, I am a simple gardener, I...

SANDRA. And you have said before how rad—

> *Sandra pulls her hand away from Max's face, accidentally tearing off one of Max's mutton chops. Max takes it back and tries to stick it back on, but it won't stick. Max swaps places with Sandra so his remaining chop is facing the audience. Little vamp here of Max grinning at the audience.*

And you have said before—

> *Max holds the loose chop up so it looks like a moustache on his face.*

And you have said before—

*Max holds up the loose chop so it looks like a moustache on Sandra's face.*

And you have said before how radiant I look as I walk across the gardens. Oh Arthur, protect me. I'll be yours if you do.

*Sandra grasps Max tightly.*

MAX. Miss Colleymoore, I do not feel as you suggest. You are a murderer and a seductress and I shall not be seduced.

*Max pushes Sandra away. Sandra lets out a squeal of frustration and bangs on the side of the clock. Trevor is startled within the clock and opens the door, knocking Sandra out again.*

*Max and Trevor look at one another. They lift Sandra's unconscious body into the clock. Having done this, they remember the audience is watching. Max looks at the script and to Trevor. He gives Trevor the script and gestures to present him to the audience. Trevor reluctantly reads as Florence.*

TREVOR. *(Reads.)* But Arthur, how can you resist me? I'm a beautiful woman.

MAX. Stop, Miss Colleymoore. You are using your powers over men as you always have.

TREVOR. *(Reads.)* You can't pretend your feelings aren't real.

MAX. Very well, perhaps it is true that I have admired you.

TREVOR. *(Reads.)* Then kiss...*ohh!* Then kiss me, Arthur. You know you want to.

*Beat. Max approaches Trevor. Trevor breaks away. He speaks to someone offstage.*

Nah. Nah. No one wants to see that.

*Vamp. Sometimes audiences become very involved here. Max looks to them for their approval that they do want to see this and is encouraged and runs over and kisses Trevor (mouth wide open over his as it was with Sandra earlier). Robert, Chris and Dennis enter and see them.*

ROBERT. What on earth is...

*Silence.*

What on earth is going on?

MAX. I can explain.

ROBERT. I don't think you can.

DENNIS. Miss Colleymoore in Arthur's arms?

CHRIS. A second affair?

ROBERT. Florence, you've changed.

TREVOR. *(Reads.)* Your wild accusations have driven me to this. I feel dizzy. I feel like I'm about to pass out!

CHRIS. I suggest you settle down, Miss Colleymoore.

DENNIS. Quickly, where's her medication?

ROBERT. Blast, I must have left it in the study.

*Robert exits through the downstairs door.*

CHRIS. Miss Colleymoore, you are a vile criminal.

DENNIS. And to think we took you in!

MAX. You have manipulated me. I have let my master down tonight.

CHRIS. And all the while you were plotting your fiancé's demise!

TREVOR. Oh Inspector! All these accusations, I feel an episode coming on.

*Trevor protests at having to do this.*

CHRIS. *(Snarling under his breath.)* Have an episode.

*Trevor reluctantly begins to have an episode. He then starts to enjoy it, playing off the audience. He builds it until his episode becomes ridiculously large and invades Chris' personal space. Chris pushes him aside, and Trevor trips under the upper level.*

Settle down, Miss Colleymoore!

*Robert reappears through the upstairs door.*

ROBERT. Now where's this medi-CATION!

*As Robert steps on the upper level, it fully collapses, crushing Trevor. Silence. Dennis bangs his fist on the chaise longue in frustration.*

If you'll excuse me.

*Robert exits and closes the door, causing a piece of lighting truss to swing down from the rig with a big spark.*

CHRIS. An adulteress and a cold-blooded killer!

SANDRA. *(Within the clock.)* I'm not, Inspector!

*All turn to face the clock. Sandra tries to get out. Chris tries to open the front, but she is stuck inside.*

CHRIS. Yes you are, Miss Colleymoore!

SANDRA. *(From within the clock.)* Oh Inspector! I can't take it anymore, I shall faint.

*Chris lowers the clock onto one side. Beat.*

DENNIS. She's fainted.

MAX. It's all become too much for her.

CHRIS. Quickly, lie her down on the chaise.

*Beat. Max, Dennis and Chris lift the clock onto the chaise longue. The legs snap.*

That's better.

*Robert enters with a pillbox and a glass of water.*

ROBERT. I found Florence's— *(Sees the clock and freezes.)* …medication… what's happened?

CHRIS. Florence has fainted.

*Chris, Max and Dennis all gesture to the clock in unison.*

MAX. There there, Miss Colleymoore.

*Dennis, Max and Chris all stroke the clock.*

ROBERT. Good Lord. I'll wake her up.

*Robert throws the glass of water onto the clock face.*

She's out cold.

CHRIS. But Arthur, is this the same person you saw outside the window this evening?

MAX. I cannot tell, Inspector. Mr. Colleymoore, please move her hands from her face.

*Robert slowly looks at the clock, then swiftly tears the hands off of the clock face and pockets them.*

It was not her, Inspector. Besides the figure I saw was that of a man.

*Annie slowly stands up in the window. Robert shoves her out of sight.*

CHRIS. Of course it was, you were taken in by a handkerchief planted outside the window to frame Florence. She and Cecil both have plausible motives for murder, but the true motive belongs to Perkins!

*Annie enters through the door, getting in between Chris and Dennis as Chris points to Dennis.*

DENNIS. Me, Inspector?

CHRIS. You, Perkins! It appears Charles made Perkins the sole beneficiary…

*Annie picks up the script in Trevor's hand, revealing a splatter of blood across the front of it.*

…of his inheritance.

DENNIS. This is all a mistake.

CHRIS. Save your…

*Annie climbs up on top of the clock to resume playing Florence. She flops down, pretending to be unconscious.*

Save your pleading for the police station.

*Chris throws a pair of handcuffs to Robert, who cuffs Dennis to the chaise longue.*

Thomas, handcuff him to the chaise longue lest he escape before I can drive him there.

MAX. That won't be for hours, the snow is at its peak.

*A single weak handful of snow is thrown in the window.*

DENNIS. It's not true, I tell you.

*Annie pretends to wake up.*

ANNIE. What happened? I must have fainted! Curse my delicate…

*Sandra opens the door of the grandfather clock, hitting Annie.*

SANDRA. What happened? I must have fainted! Curse my delicate constitution.

ROBERT. You did faint, Florence. We've learned that Perkins committed the murder.

SANDRA. Perkins?

ANNIE. *(Copying Sandra.)* Perkins?

SANDRA and ANNIE. But he's such a kindly old man!

> *Sandra and Annie small vamp telling each other to get off stage. They both freeze in Florence's position s. l.*

DENNIS. This is all a misunderstanding! I didn't kill Charles, but I know who did.

ALL. WHO?

DENNIS. INSPECTOR CARTER!

> *All gasp.*

MAX. What on earth?

CHRIS. Poppycock!

DENNIS. You did it because Charles knew about the police money you were *(Checks hand.)* embezzling. *(Pronounced "em-bee-zeling.")*

CHRIS. Nonsense!

DENNIS. You say you'd met before, that he was a consultant on a fraud case you were working on.

CHRIS. What of it?

DENNIS. Charles found the reason why no arrests had been made is because the man committing the crime was yourself. You were the *(Checks hand.)* facade. *(Pronounced "fu-cayde." Checks his other hand.)* The perpetrator. You were the perpetrator.

CHRIS. You can't prove it.

MAX. But Charley could and that's why you killed him.

CHRIS. Never!

DENNIS. I know your secret, Inspector. What will you do? Kill me too?

> *Chris draws a gun and points it at Dennis.*

CHRIS. I will, confound it.

SANDRA and ANNIE. What a devil of a situation this is!

> *Jonathan enters through the downstairs door, again holding his gun.*

JONATHAN. Not so fast, Inspector!

*All gasp.*

ROBERT. Charles!

CHRIS. Haversham!

DENNIS and MAX. Sir!

ANNIE. Charley! I—

SANDRA. *(Pushes in front.)* Charley! I thought you were dead.

CHRIS. You're alive? It's not possible.

JONATHAN. Oh, I'm afraid it is. You couldn't kill me that easily.

CHRIS. How did you survive?

JONATHAN. I simply didn't drink the poisoned sherry you left out for me this evening.

ANNIE. Charley—

*Sandra stamps on Annie's foot.*

SANDRA. Charley, this is all more than I can bear!

JONATHAN. Ever since we last spoke at the police station it was clear you thought I was on to you. It was at this point I became afraid you might try to kill me. For months now I've had my guard up and tonight you fell into my trap.

DENNIS. You've been hiding in the grounds ever since this afternoon when you planted the poison.

MAX. It was you that I saw. You were the mysterious figure!

SANDRA and ANNIE. I thought it was strange…

*Annie pushes the bookcase, which swivels and swallows Sandra. Annie then blocks Sandra from coming back in.*

ANNIE. *I thought it was strange you got here so quickly in such terrible weather!*

*Sandra gives up on the bookcase and falls silent. Annie wanders over to the window, picking up a tray.*

MAX. But what about the handkerchief bearing Florence Colleymoore's initials?

JONATHAN. Perhaps you should ask Inspector Carter, or should I say Inspector Frederick Carter.

ALL. *F.C.*

MAX. The same initials.

DENNIS. Precisely, and after committing the crime you found Charles' will in his ledger and tried to pin the whole thing on me.

*Sandra appears through the window.*

SANDRA. You damned—

*Annie hits Sandra with the tray. Sandra falls out of sight behind the window.*

ANNIE. You damned crafty devil!

JONATHAN. Crafty indeed. Perkins here is as innocent as I am. Remove those handcuffs this instant!

ROBERT. Of course, Charles, I have the key.

*Robert goes to release Dennis, but he doesn't have the key. Robert searches his pockets for the key. Dennis remains handcuffed to the chaise longue. Robert and Max try to pull the handcuffs off. Sandra is seen getting up behind the window and running to the downstairs door, but Annie gets there first and holds it shut.*

JONATHAN. Drop the gun, Inspector.

SANDRA. *(Entering, but Annie pushes the door shut on her.)* Ay / me!

ANNIE. Ay me!

CHRIS. Never! I came here to kill you, Charles, and I won't leave until the job's done.

JONATHAN. It's over, Inspector. I could prove your guilt in a second. I have the evidence upstairs in the safe in my study. Fetch the papers, Perkins.

DENNIS. Yes, sir.

*Robert, Dennis and Max all look up. Dennis is still handcuffed to the chaise longue. Robert and Max quickly lift the clock off of the chaise longue and Dennis, Chris and Jonathan carry the chaise longue over towards the fallen study floor so Dennis can fetch the papers. Robert and Max place the clock D.S. C.*

JONATHAN. Lower your weapon, Inspector. It's over.

CHRIS. What are you going to do, Charles? Shoot me in front of a room full of witnesses?

JONATHAN. Don't think I wouldn't do it, Carter. You tried to kill me; I'd merely be returning the favour.

ANNIE. Please, Inspector, you're frightening me!

> *Sandra's hand is seen trying to reach around the door, but Annie slams it shut. Sandra screams and then magically Sandra bursts out of the clock.*

SANDRA. Please, Inspector, you're frightening me!

> *Annie is furious, the others all amazed.*

CHRIS. You ought to be frightened!

JONATHAN. Arthur, hold everyone in this room. I'll send a wire to the local police.

MAX. Yes, sir.

> *Jonathan hands Max his gun and exits through the downstairs door.*

ANNIE and SANDRA. You monster! You tried to kill Charles and you killed Ce…

> *Annie charges at Sandra, but Sandra moves out of the way and Annie charges out through the window.*

SANDRA. …and you killed Cecil. How could you?!

> *Sandra stands back in front of the window, but Annie leans in and drags her out through it so she lands on her back on the floor behind. Annie then dives onto Sandra elbow first. We hear them continuing to fight behind the set.*

CHRIS. Alright I admit it, I tried to kill Charles, but I couldn't have done it without the help of my accomplice.

MAX. Your accomplice?

> *Robert rushes to the door and tries to get out.*

CHRIS. That's right. Thomas Colleymoore!

> *Robert arrives at the door.*

ROBERT. It's true—

71

*Max turns quickly, and the barrel of the gun flies off, narrowly missing Robert.*

*It's true!* I'm the Inspector's accomplice; I helped him move the money. But don't you think for one second I'm going down for this. Good God! Charley's locked the door.

*The door comes off its hinges in Robert's hand.*

We're trapped!

*Robert ditches the door offstage.*

CHRIS. Quickly, Colleymoore! Get in the elevator. We can escape down the east staircase.

MAX. Get away from the elevator you two. Winston, get him, boy!

*Max throws the lead at Chris, who screams as if under attack by Winston.*

CHRIS. Down, Winston!

*Chris throws the lead out of the window. Jonathan bursts in through the upper-level door.*

JONATHAN. Now to send that telegra-*aaaahh!*

*Jonathan falls off the edge, grabs on to the broken truss and swings right across the stage, sending Chris, Robert and Max flying like skittles. Jonathan lands in front of the downstairs doorway, trembling.*

CHRIS. Quickly, Colleymoore, we can escape through the study.

*Dennis slides back down the upper-level floor, still hand-cuffed to the chaise longue and now carrying the papers.*

DENNIS. The papers, sir.

*Dennis throws the papers to Jonathan.*

JONATHAN. Thank you, Perkins, now fetch my reading glasses from the library.

DENNIS. Yes, sir.

*Dennis carries the chaise out through the door.*

ROBERT. Get out of my way, Charles.

*Robert runs up the upper level and manages to get into the study doorway at the top.*

CHRIS. Push him aside, Colleymoore. Do you want to spend the rest of your life in jail?

> *Chris runs up the upper level, grabs Robert's foot for support but slides back down to the floor, pulling Robert with him.*

ROBERT. I will strike you down, Char-*ley!*

CHRIS. It's useless, Colleymoore, there's no way out.

> *Sandra runs back in.*

SANDRA. Brother, I'm surprised at—

> *Annie appears in the window with the ledger and hits Sandra in the stomach and then over the head with it.*

ANNIE. Brother, I'm surprised at you. I don't know what you've become!

> *Annie jumps in through the window and over Sandra.*

ROBERT. *(Getting to his feet.)* I feel so ashamed. Carter and I found that between the two of us we could steal money from the police's sundry accounts easily. Carter had access and I had the facility to move the money fast and keep it secure, or so I thought until earlier on this evening…

> *Robert forgets his line. Trevor emerges from below the collapsed upper level, looking badly injured. He staggers towards the door.*

Line!

TREVOR. This set's a damn death trap!

> *Trevor shuffles off through the door.*

ROBERT. This set's a damn death trap!

CHRIS. *(Prompts Robert.)* As for Cecil!

ROBERT. As for Cecil, that was more a crime of passion, simple as that.

JONATHAN. Now I hold in my hand a written list of every fraudulent transaction Thomas Colleymoore and Inspector Carter made.

SANDRA and ANNIE. No this can't be true, I can't belie—

> *Sandra throws the vase at Annie. Annie ducks and the vase smashes against the back wall.*

SANDRA.  I can't believe it!

JONATHAN.  Florence, your sordid affair made me sick. It broke my heart.

> *Annie and Sandra both try and get hold of Jonathan to continue the scene, pulling him to the floor in the process.*

SANDRA and ANNIE.  Charley! Look at me the way you used to look at me!

> *Vamp. Annie and Sandra each trying to shout the line over the other. Robert and Chris try to pull them apart, but Annie takes Robert out with a swift punch to the groin. She goes to punch Sandra, but Sandra ducks and Annie hits Chris in the chest, sending him down as well. Dennis reappears in the doorway, holding Charles' reading glasses.*

DENNIS.  *(Over the shouting.)* Your reading glasses, sir!

JONATHAN.  *(Over the shouting.)* Thank you, Perkins!

> *Doorbell sounds.*

Get the door, Perkins.

DENNIS.  Yes, sir!!

> *Dennis exits, still with the chaise longue in tow.*

SANDRA.  Charley!

JONATHAN.  That will be the police to arrest you both.

> *Annie grabs Sandra's ankles and drags her out through the door.*

Silence, Florence, you mean nothing to me now.

SANDRA.  *(Managing to stand up.)* This is the worst night of my life!

> *Annie punches Sandra in the face; she falls out of sight behind the window.*

ANNIE.  *No! This is the worst night of my life!*

MAX.  I think this is the worst night of all of our lives.

> *Annie goes through the door, appears in the window and stamps on Sandra before ducking out of sight. Max exits.*

JONATHAN.  But Thomas, Carter had you fooled, didn't he?

ROBERT.  What do you mean?

JONATHAN. He never intended to share the money with you! Let me summarize—

ANNIE. *(Through the window.)* I love you, Charley! *(Ducks down again.)*

JONATHAN. Inspector Carter knew I discovered you and he were both embezzling police money, so you hatched a plan to kill me, planting cyanide in my sherry for me / to drink.

*Sandra appears, holding Annie back.*

SANDRA. I've still got the ring, Charley! We can make it work!

*Annie slaps Sandra, who falls out of sight. Annie fetches the tray and starts hitting Sandra with it behind the window.*

JONATHAN. Then mistakenly believing I was dead, Inspector Carter tried to pin my murder on my brother Cecil and Florence because of their affair. That is until your accomplice Thomas blundered in and shot my brother Cecil. Carter then tried to pin my murder on Perkins instead after finding my will in the ledger.

*Annie appears, tearing a strip of industrial tape off of a roll.*

ANNIE. TAKE ME, CHARLEY! IF YOU KNOW WHAT'S GOOD FOR YOU!

*Sandra stands and headbutts Annie. We hear an almighty crack, and they both collapse and fall silent behind the window.*

JONATHAN. Except what you didn't know, Thomas, was that Inspector Carter made a nine-thousand-pound withdrawal from your private accounts this morning and after framing someone for my murder he intended to flee with a one-way ticket to Dover, taking every penny with him! I think it's time to have a look inside your attaché case, Inspector, where we shall find...

*Jonathan throws the case to Robert, who opens it and produces a small green bottle.*

The bottle of cyanide.

*Robert produces a bundle of banknotes.*

Thomas Colleymoore's nine thousand pounds.

ROBERT. And of course, your one-way ticket to—

*Robert produces a Duran Duran CD box set from the attaché*

*case. Robert angrily turns to Trevor, who has reappeared in his tech box.*

*Duran Duran!!*\*

JONATHAN.  He allowed you to take all the risk by storing the stolen money in your private accounts. Isn't that right, Inspector?

CHRIS.  Alright, it's—

*Annie triumphantly makes it back onstage and poses.*

Alright, it's—

*Sandra appears in the window, tied up with tape.*

Alright, it's true! I forged your signature at the bank and took out every penny. I had intended to flee after I'd managed to frame someone for the murder. I hadn't bargained on your accountant catching on this quickly and telephoning you so soon.

*Robert runs at Chris, seizes his gun and points it at him.*

ROBERT.  You rogue! I trusted you, Carter. You made a mistake there and I'm afraid it's your last.

CHRIS.  No!

*Robert fires the gun. It doesn't fire. Robert tries the gun again, nothing.*

BANG!

*Chris falls to the floor. Robert lowers the gun to his side, where it explodes loudly, hurting his hand.*

ROBERT.  ARGH!!

DENNIS.  The officers are waiting in the hall, si—

*Dennis enters through the downstairs door, knocking over the whole door flat with the chaise longue. Robert moves back, colliding with the fireplace flat, sending that over as well. The s. l. flat falls, and Chris just manages to roll out of the way. Lastly the window flat falls down as well, leaving Annie standing in the window frame and revealing Max standing on a small stepladder, holding a bucket of snow. Silence. Stillness. Max throws a handful of snow.*

---

\* If music by a different band is used on pages 45 and 78, change the CD box set prop and the line *"Duran Duran!!"* appropriately.

JONATHAN. Excellent. Perkins, if you could please escort Miss Colleymoore downstairs. I wish to have a word with Thomas in private.

DENNIS. Yes, sir.

> *Dennis and Annie stay, trapped in by the fallen flats. Chris stares blankly at the devastation.*

JONATHAN. *(Whispers to Chris.)* You're dead.

> *Chris remembers where he is, lets out a thin cry and drops down dead.*

*(To Annie.)* Downstairs, Florence, downstairs.

> *Annie and Dennis pretend to walk downstairs on the spot where they are standing.*

Thomas! You're not the man I knew at Eton, you've become greedy and jealous.

ROBERT. *(Traumatised.)* I'm sorry, Charles, my nerves are in shreds.

JONATHAN. There's a glass of sherry by the telephone.

ROBERT. Thank you, Charles. Ever the kind host.

JONATHAN. Drink it up.

ROBERT. Most kind.

> *Robert drinks the sherry.*

JONATHAN. Tell me, Thomas, one last thing.

ROBERT. Anything, Charles. I'll tell no more lies.

JONATHAN. The glass of poisoned sherry the Inspector left out for me; what do you suppose I did with it?

ROBERT. Well, I don't…know. What do you mean? You don't mean you gave me… Charley? Charley, no! *(Forgets his line.)* Line!

TREVOR. *(From the tech box.)* Just die already!

ROBERT. Just die alread—how dare you!

> *Robert dies. A large, flamboyant death that takes him quite a way away from the table. Just as he is almost finished, Robert realises he is still holding the empty sherry glass and groans and crawls back in the other direction so he can put it down on the table. He places down the glass and drops*

*down dead. Max throws a handful of snow. Jonathan moves centre. The lights fade and a spot comes up on Jonathan.*

JONATHAN.  Oh how I wish this could have ended differently. Thomas, your lies and deceits have led you inexorably to this end. If men allow their conscience to be governed by avarice then death and destruction shall prevail. Betrayed by my brother—

*A short burst of an English new wave song like "Rio" by Duran Duran plays.*\*

TREVOR.  *(Back in his box.)* Oh come on!

*Trevor hits a button on his computer and the correct dramatic closing music plays.*

JONATHAN.  Cuckolded by my fiancée and almost murdered by my oldest friend. Let us hope we never again see…a murder at Haversham Manor.

*The chandelier hanging above the space suddenly sparks and crashes down onto Jonathan. The lights black out just before it hits him.*

### End of Play

---

\* See Note on Songs/Recordings at the back of this volume.

## PROPERTY LIST
*(Use this space to create props lists for your production)*

# SOUND EFFECTS
*(Use this space to create sound effects lists for your production)*

**Dear reader,**

Thank you for supporting playwrights by purchasing this acting edition! You may not know that Dramatists Play Service was founded, in 1936, by the Dramatists Guild and a number of prominent play agents to protect the rights and interests of playwrights. To this day, we are still a small company committed to our partnership with the Guild, and by proxy all playwrights, established and aspiring, working in the English language.

Because of our status as a small, independent publisher, we respectfully reiterate that this text may not be distributed or copied in any way, or uploaded to any file-sharing sites, including ones you might think are private. Photocopying or electronically distributing books means both DPS and the playwright are not paid for the work, and that ultimately hurts playwrights everywhere, as our profits are shared with the Guild.

We also hope you want to perform this play! Plays are wonderful to read, but even better when seen. If you are interested in performing or producing the play, please be aware that performance rights must be obtained through Dramatists Play Service. This is true for *any* public performance, even if no one is getting paid or admission is not being charged. Again, playwrights often make their sole living from performance royalties, so performing plays without paying the royalty is ultimately a loss for a real writer.

This acting edition is the **only approved text for performance**. There may be other editions of the play available for sale from other publishers, but DPS has worked closely with the playwright to ensure this published text reflects their desired text of all future productions. If you have purchased a revised edition (sometimes referred to as other types of editions, like "Broadway Edition," or "[Year] Edition"), that is the only edition you may use for performance, unless explicitly stated in writing by Dramatists Play Service.

Finally, this script cannot be changed without written permission from Dramatists Play Service. If a production intends to change the script in any way—including casting against the writer's intentions for characters, removing or changing "bad" words, or making other cuts however small—without permission, they are breaking the law. And, perhaps more importantly, changing an artist's work. Please don't do that!

We are thrilled that this play has made it into your hands. We hope you love it as much as we do, and thank you for helping us keep the American theater alive and vital.

## Note on Songs/Recordings, Images, or Other Production Design Elements

Be advised that Dramatists Play Service, Inc., neither holds the rights to nor grants permission to use any songs, recordings, images, or other design elements mentioned in the play. It is the responsibility of the producing theater/organization to obtain permission of the copyright owner(s) for any such use. Additional royalty fees may apply for the right to use copyrighted materials.

For any songs/recordings, images, or other design elements mentioned in the play, works in the public domain may be substituted. It is the producing theater/organization's responsibility to ensure the substituted work is indeed in the public domain. Dramatists Play Service, Inc., cannot advise as to whether or not a song/arrangement/recording, image, or other design element is in the public domain.

## Additional Copyright Information

## Notice to Professional Licensees Interested in Presenting a Version of the Tony® Award-winning Broadway and West End Production of the Play

Without prejudice to the above notice, the above rights and digital and physical resources to realise the contributions are available on a basis to suit a wide variety of production capabilities of professional licensees of the Play upon application to Mischief Worldwide Ltd. at www.mischiefworldwide.com.

# NOTES
*(Use this space to make notes for your production)*

# NOTES
*(Use this space to make notes for your production)*

# NOTES
*(Use this space to make notes for your production)*